GODSMACK

Arranged by Jordan Baker

ISBN 1-4234-0794-6

Visit Hal Leonard Online at www.halleonard.com

HAL•LEONARD®
CORPORATION
7777 W. BLUEMOUND RD. P.O. BOX 13819
MILWAUKEE, WISCONSIN 53213

Guitar Notation Legend

THE MUSICAL STAFF shows pitches and rhythms and is divided by bar lines into measures. Pitches are named after the first seven letters of the alphabet.

TABLATURE graphically represents the guitar fingerboard. Each horizontal line represents a string, and each number represents a fret.

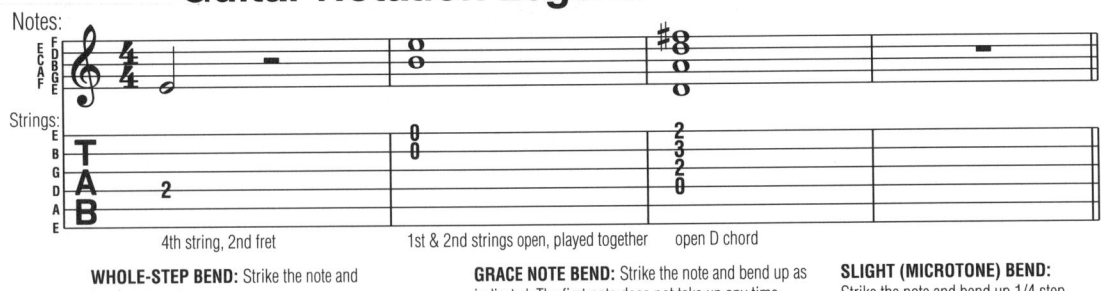

4th string, 2nd fret   1st & 2nd strings open, played together   open D chord

HALF-STEP BEND: Strike the note and bend up 1/2 step.

WHOLE-STEP BEND: Strike the note and bend up one step.

GRACE NOTE BEND: Strike the note and bend up as indicated. The first note does not take up any time.

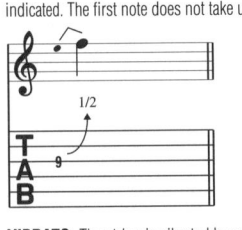

SLIGHT (MICROTONE) BEND: Strike the note and bend up 1/4 step.

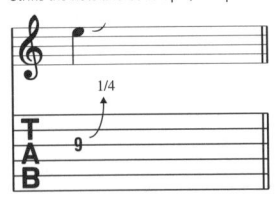

BEND AND RELEASE: Strike the note and bend up as indicated, then release back to the original note. Only the first note is struck.

PRE-BEND: Bend the note as indicated, then strike it.

VIBRATO: The string is vibrated by rapidly bending and releasing the note with the fretting hand.

PALM MUTING: The note is partially muted by the pick hand lightly touching the string(s) just before the bridge.

HAMMER-ON: Strike the first (lower) note with one finger, then sound the higher note (on the same string) with another finger by fretting it without picking.

PULL-OFF: Place both fingers on the notes to be sounded. Strike the first note and without picking, pull the finger off to sound the second (lower) note.

LEGATO SLIDE: Strike the first note and then slide the same fret-hand finger up or down to the second note. The second note is not struck.

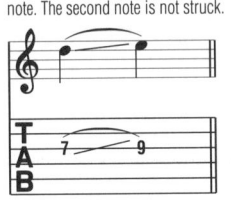

SHIFT SLIDE: Same as legato slide, except the second note is struck.

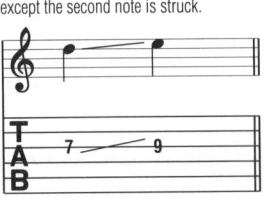

TRILL: Very rapidly alternate between the notes indicated by continuously hammering on and pulling off.

TAPPING: Hammer ("tap") the fret indicated with the pick-hand index or middle finger and pull off to the note fretted by the fret hand.

NATURAL HARMONIC: Strike the note while the fret-hand lightly touches the string directly over the fret indicated.

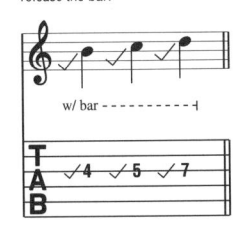

PINCH HARMONIC: The note is fretted normally and a harmonic is produced by adding the edge of the thumb or the tip of the index finger of the pick hand to the normal pick attack.

TREMOLO PICKING: The note is picked as rapidly and continuously as possible.

VIBRATO BAR DIVE AND RETURN: The pitch of the note or chord is dropped a specified number of steps (in rhythm) then returned to the original pitch.

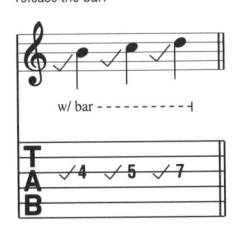

VIBRATO BAR SCOOP: Depress the bar just before striking the note, then quickly release the bar.

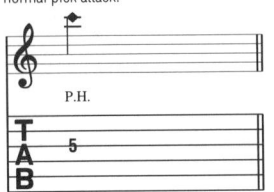

VIBRATO BAR DIP: Strike the note and then immediately drop a specified number of steps, then release back to the original pitch.

Additional Musical Definitions

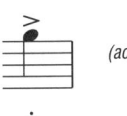

(accent) • Accentuate note (play it louder)

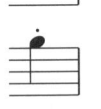

(staccato) • Play the note short

D.S. al Coda • Go back to the sign (𝄋), then play until the measure marked ***"To Coda,"*** then skip to the section labelled ***"Coda."***

D.C. al Fine • Go back to the beginning of the song and play until the measure marked ***"Fine"*** (end).

Fill • Label used to identify a brief melodic figure which is to be inserted into the arrangement.

N.C. • Instrument is silent (drops out).

• Repeat measures between signs.

1. 2. • When a repeated section has different endings, play the first ending only the first time and the second ending only the second time.

GODSMACK

HAL•LEONARD GUITAR PLAY-ALONG®

VOL. 59

CONTENTS

Awake

Words and Music by Sully Erna

Drop D tuning, down 1 step:
(low to high) C-G-C-F-A-D

Intro

Moderate Rock ♩ = 110

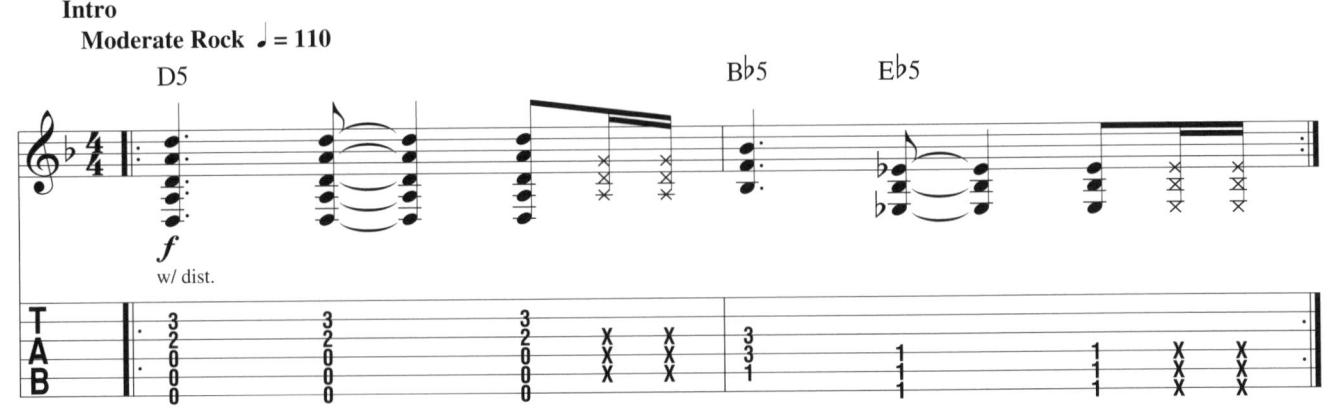

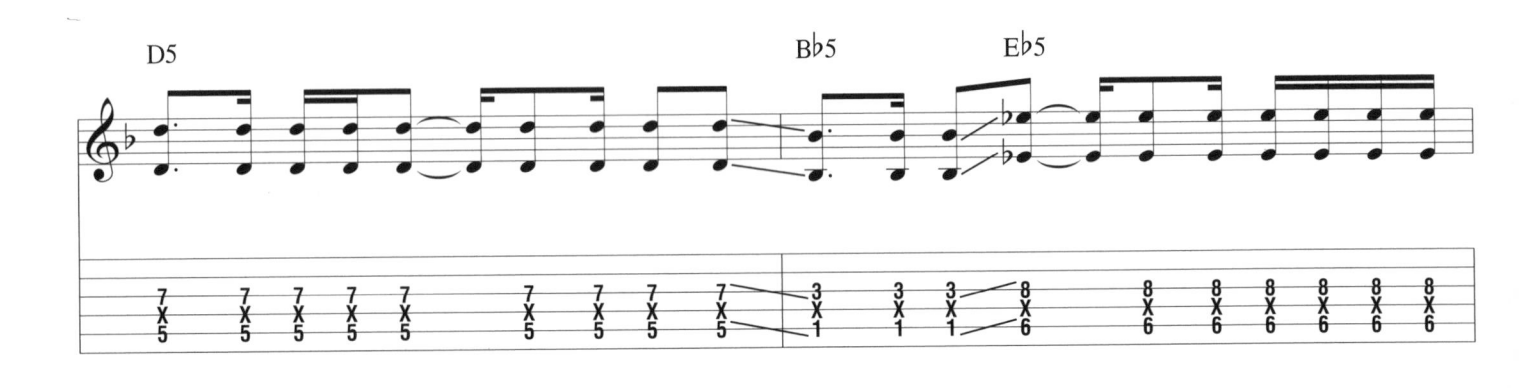

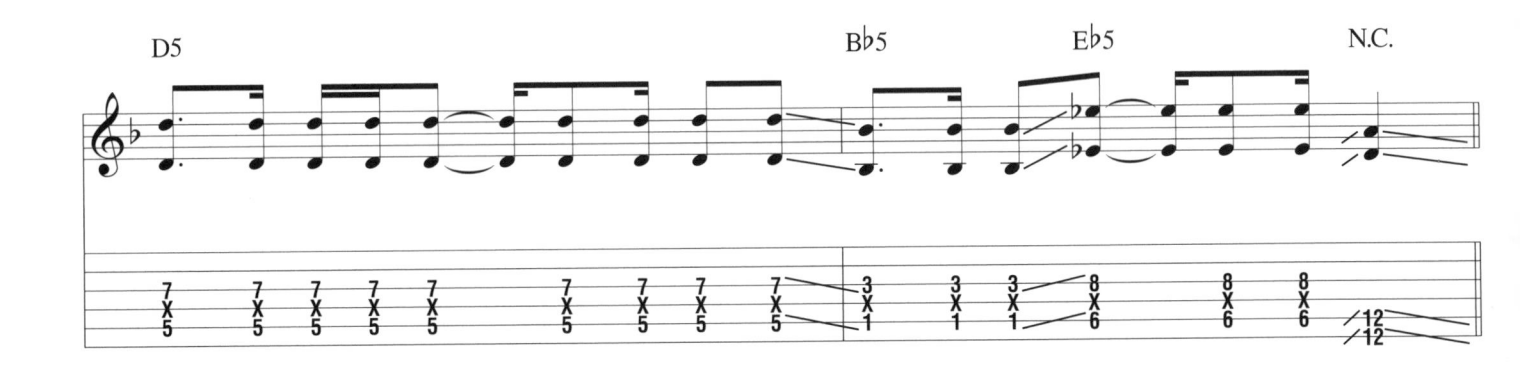

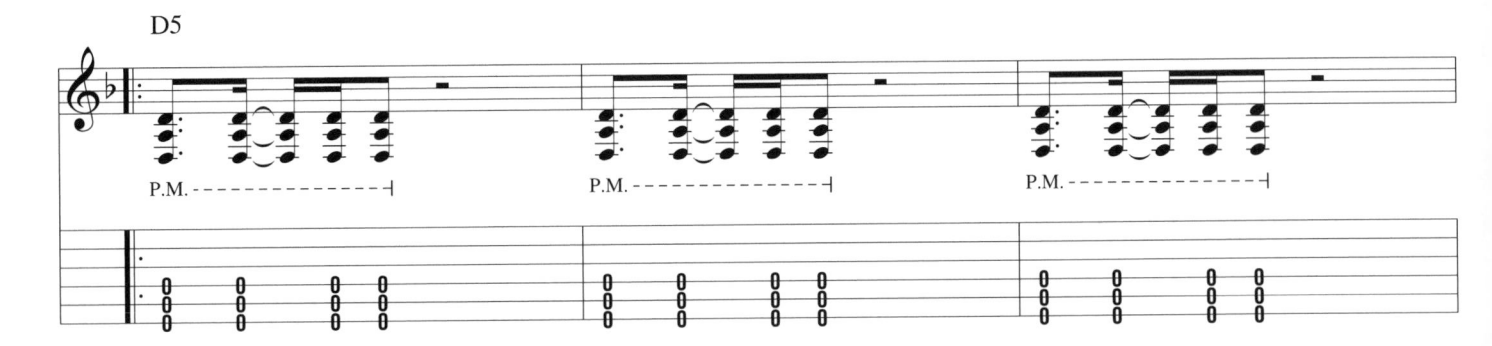

Verse

D5

1. Wait an - oth - er min - ute. Can't you ___ see what this pain ___ has ___ fuck - ing
2. *See additional lyrics*

Bb5   Eb5   D5

done to ___ me? ___ I'm ___ a - live ___ and ___ still kick-ing. What you ___ see, I can see and

%⃣ **Chorus**
3rd time, substitute Fill 2

Bb5   Eb5   D5

may - be, ___ ah, you'll think be - fore you ___ speak. ___ I'm ___ a - live

Fill 2

wah-wah off

(15)   (15)

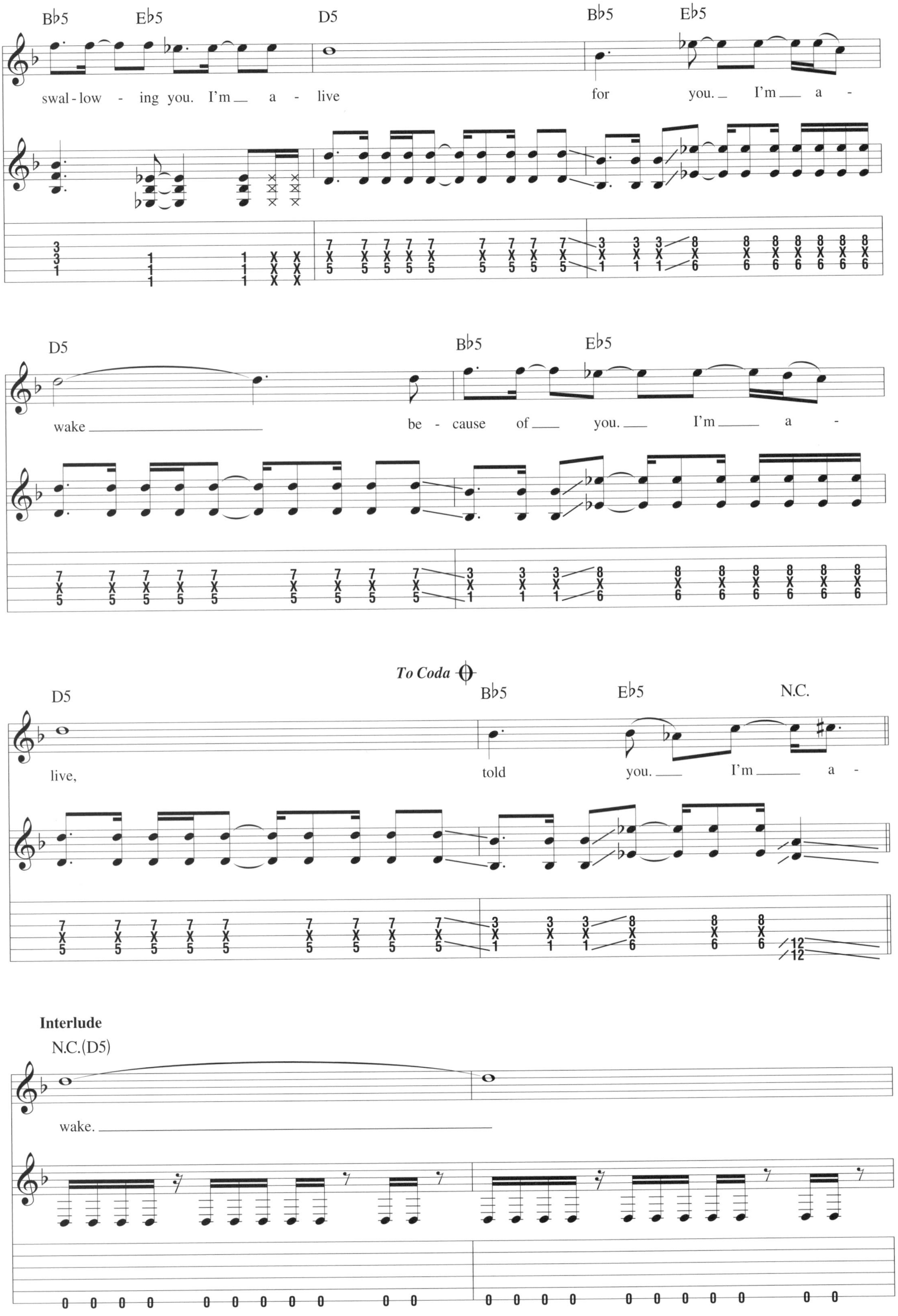
Bb5
Eb5
D5
Bb5
Eb5
swal - low - ing you. I'm a - live
for you. I'm a -
D5
Bb5
Eb5
wake
be - cause of you. I'm a -
To Coda
D5
Bb5
Eb5
N.C.
live,
told you. I'm a -
Interlude
N.C.(D5)
wake.

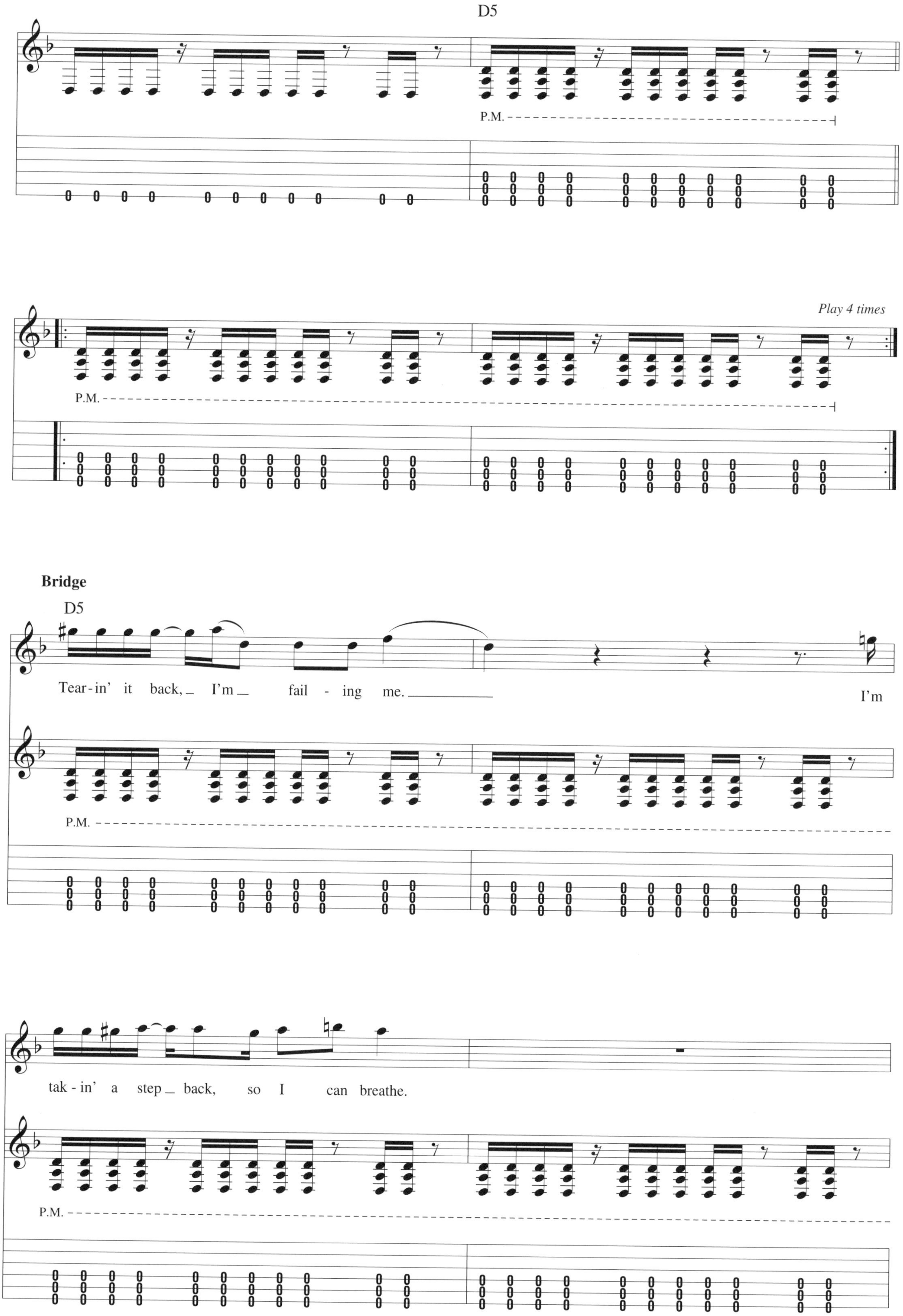
D5
P.M.
Play 4 times
P.M.
Bridge
D5
Tear-in' it back, I'm fail - ing me. I'm
P.M.
tak - in' a step back, so I can breathe.
P.M.

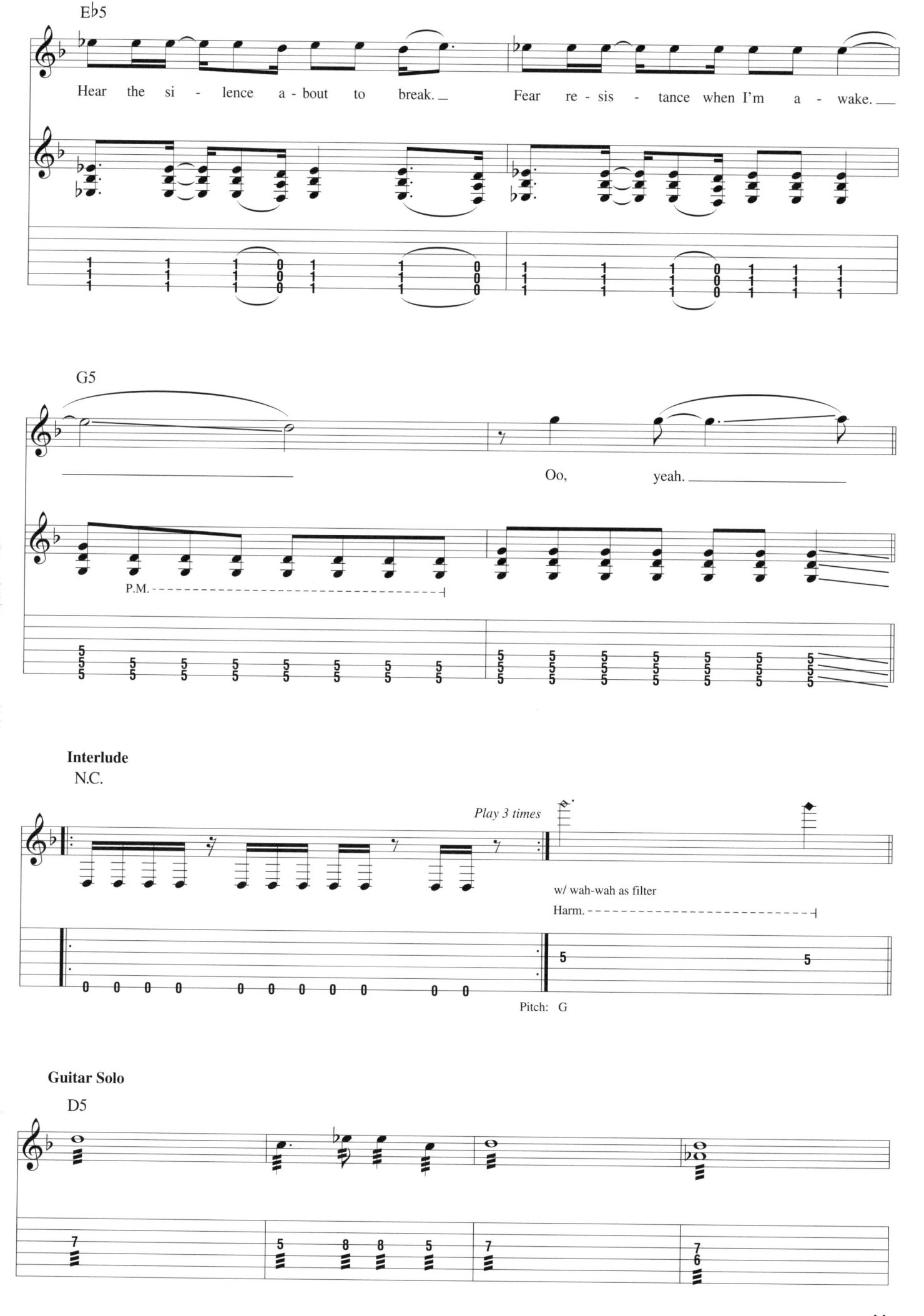

Coda

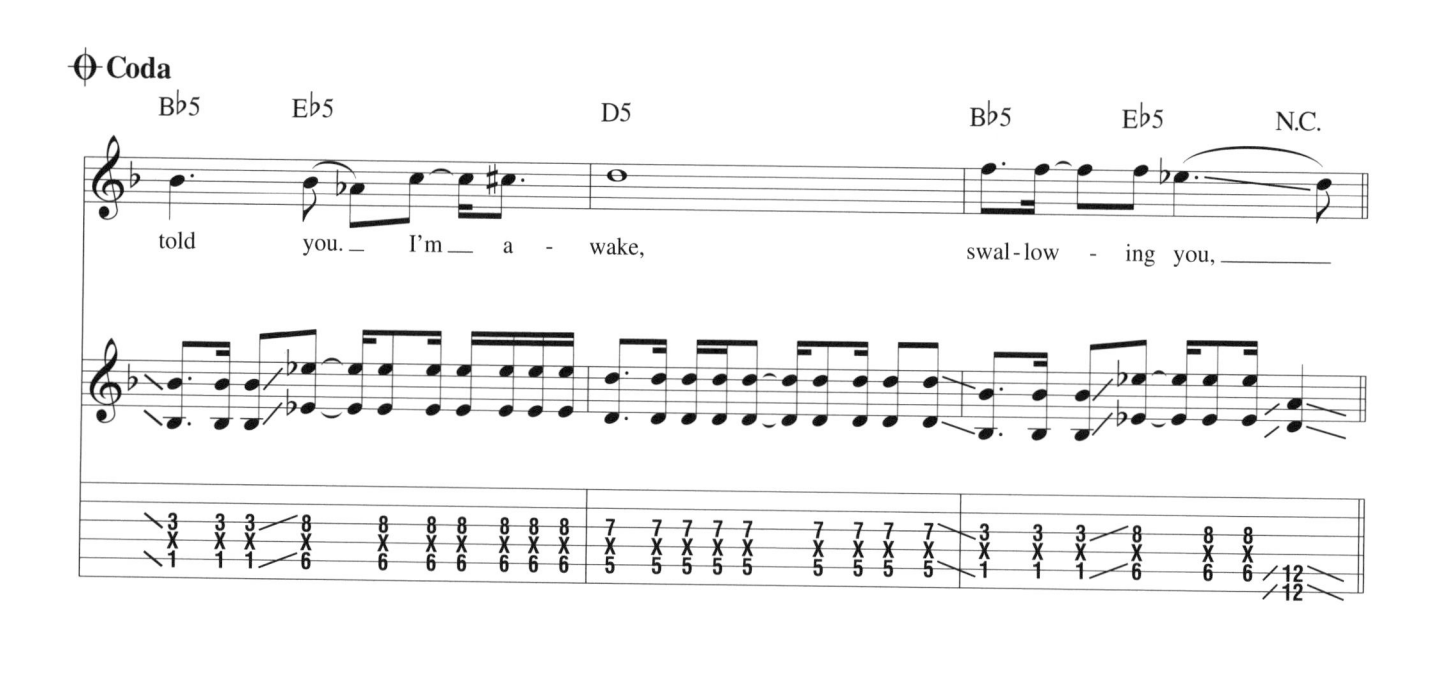

told you.__ I'm__ a - wake, swal-low - ing you,_____

Outro

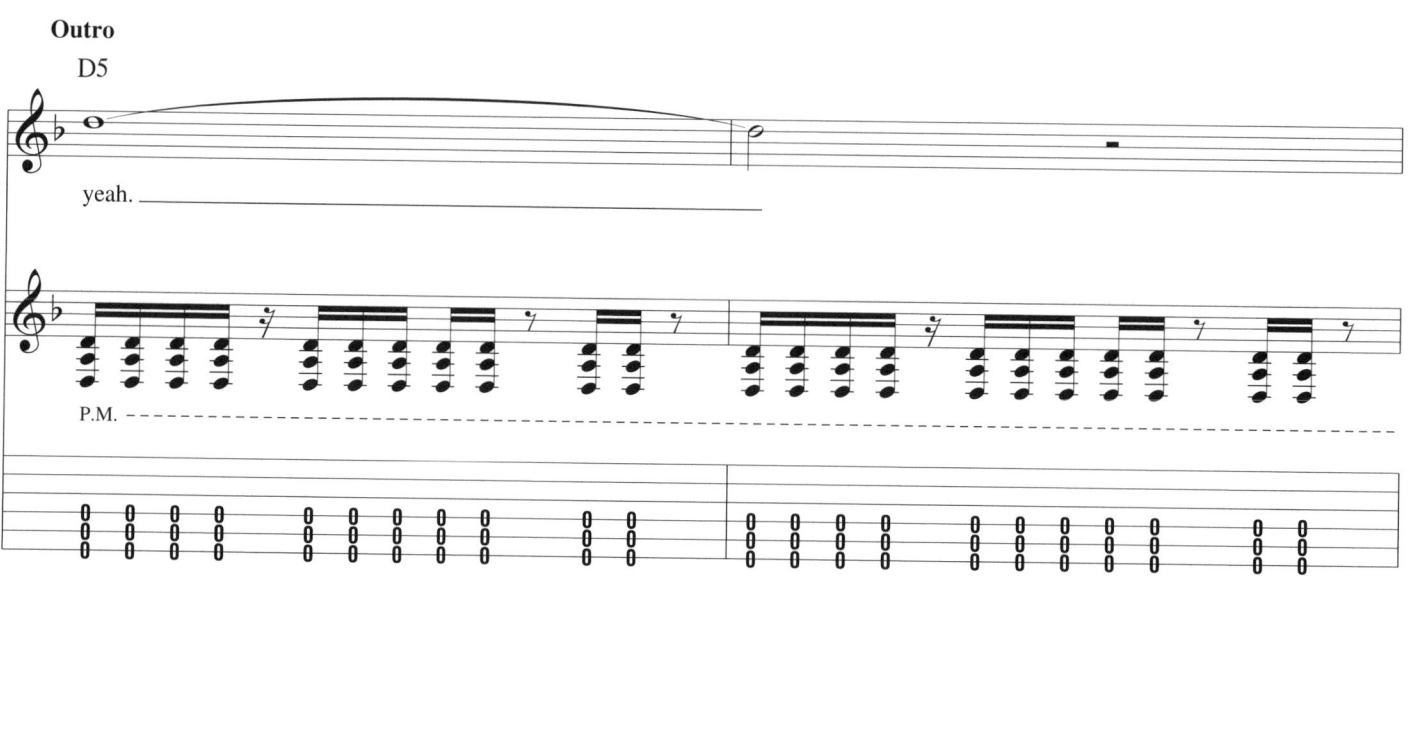

yeah._____

Additional Lyrics

2. Take another second.
Turn your back on me and
Make believe that you're always happy.
It's safe to say you're never alive.
A big part of you has died, and by the way,
I hope you're satisfied.

Bad Religion

Words and Music by Sully Erna and Tommy Stewart

Drop D tuning:
(low to high) D-A-D-G-B-E

Intro
Fast Rock ♩ = 154

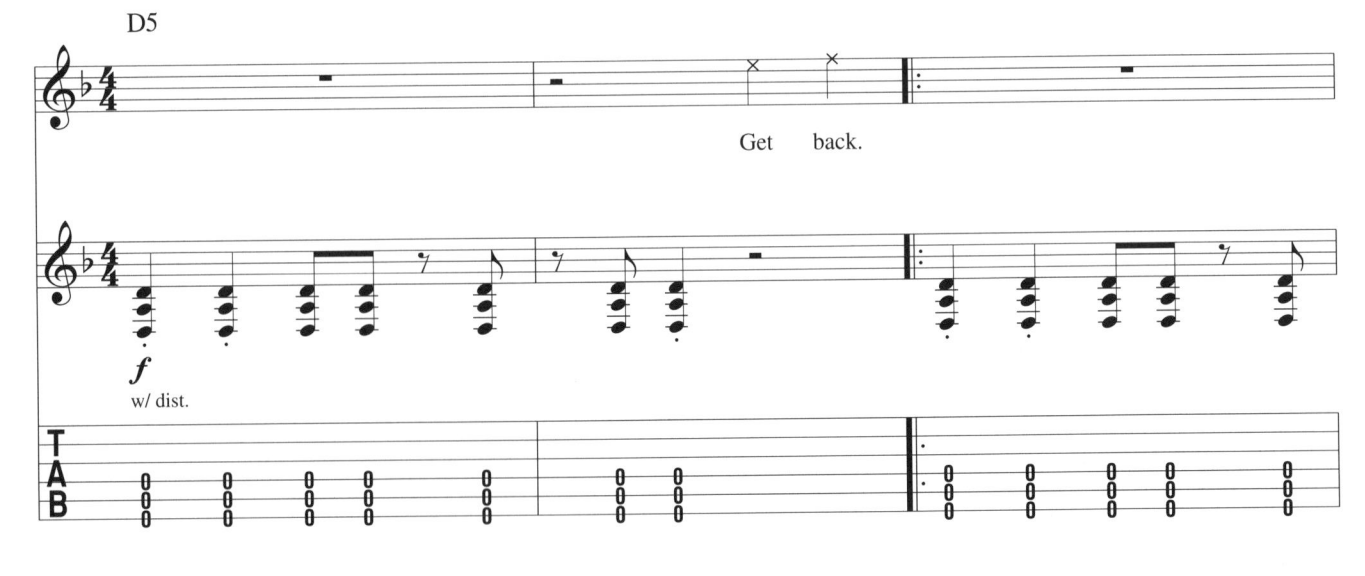

Get back.

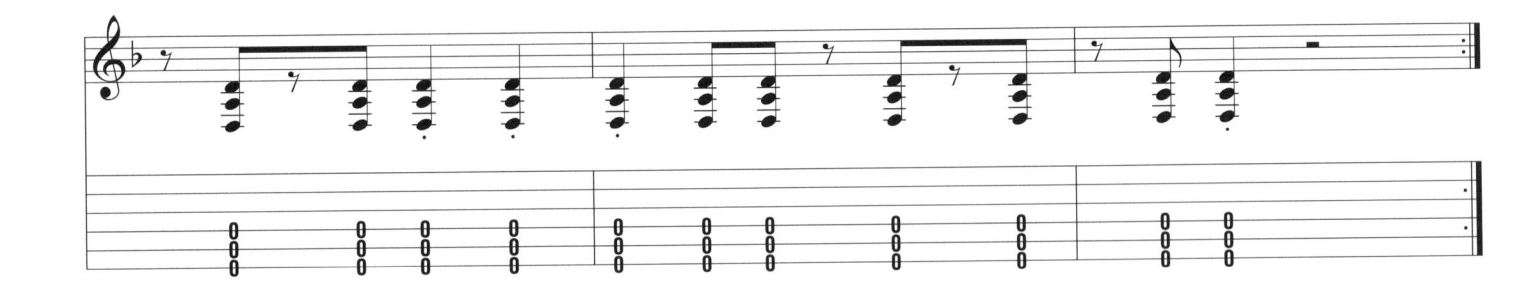

Verse
D5

1. Can __ you __ feel _____ I'm not like __ you __ an - y-more?
2. *See additional lyrics*

I can't ___ see, _____ I can't breathe. ___

See you ___ quiv - er like the dogs ___ on ___ the _____ streets.

Look - ing ___ down _____ on as I beat ___ you. Oh, it's a

Chorus
Half-time feel

D5   C5   D5

bad ___ re - li - gion, _____ from a bro - ken na - tion. ___

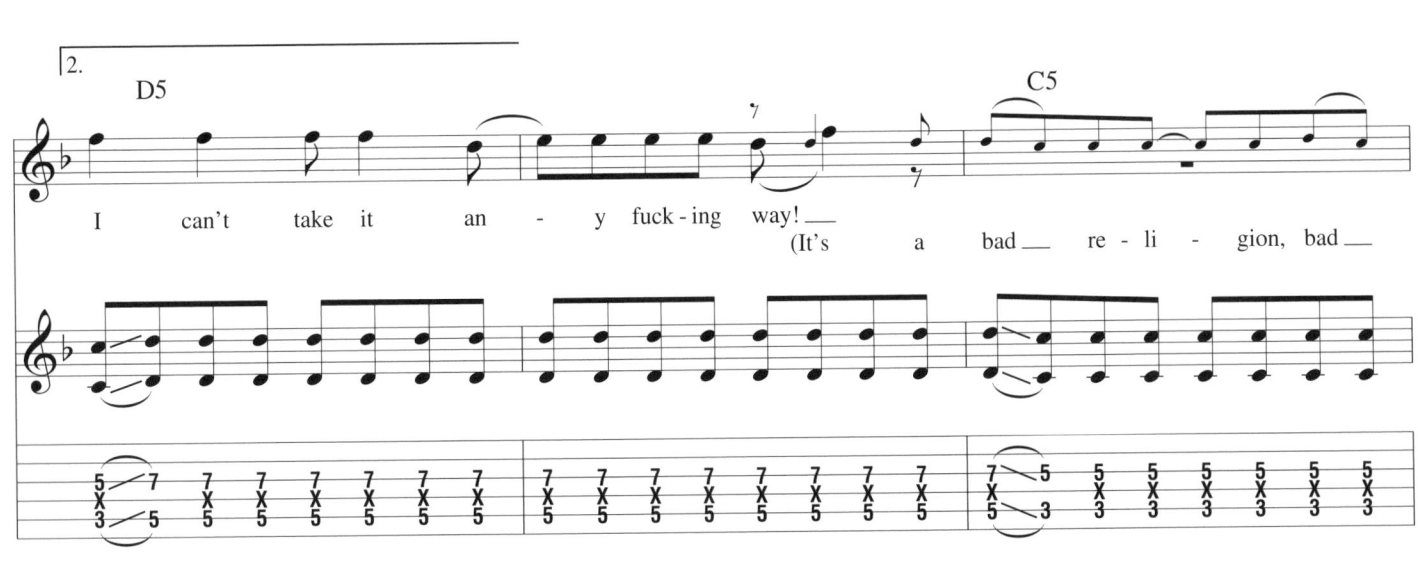

C5

It's a con - tra - dic - tion, _____ and

1.

End half-time feel

D5

I can't take it an - y - more, yeah.

2.

D5   **C5**

I can't take it an - y fuck - ing way! ___ (It's a bad ___ re - li - gion, bad ___

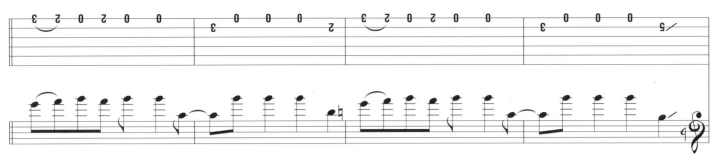

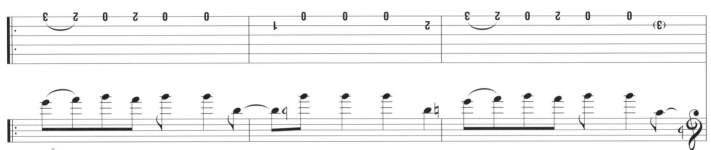

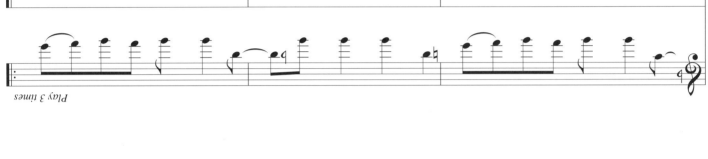

Outro

Yeah.

Additional Lyrics

2. Who's to say I won't like you anyway?
   Take a deep breath, I'm alive.
   Can you hear me? I'm alive inside of you.
   Agony creeps up behind you.

Greed

Words and Music by Sully Erna

Drop D tuning, down 1 step:
(low to high) C-G-C-F-A-D

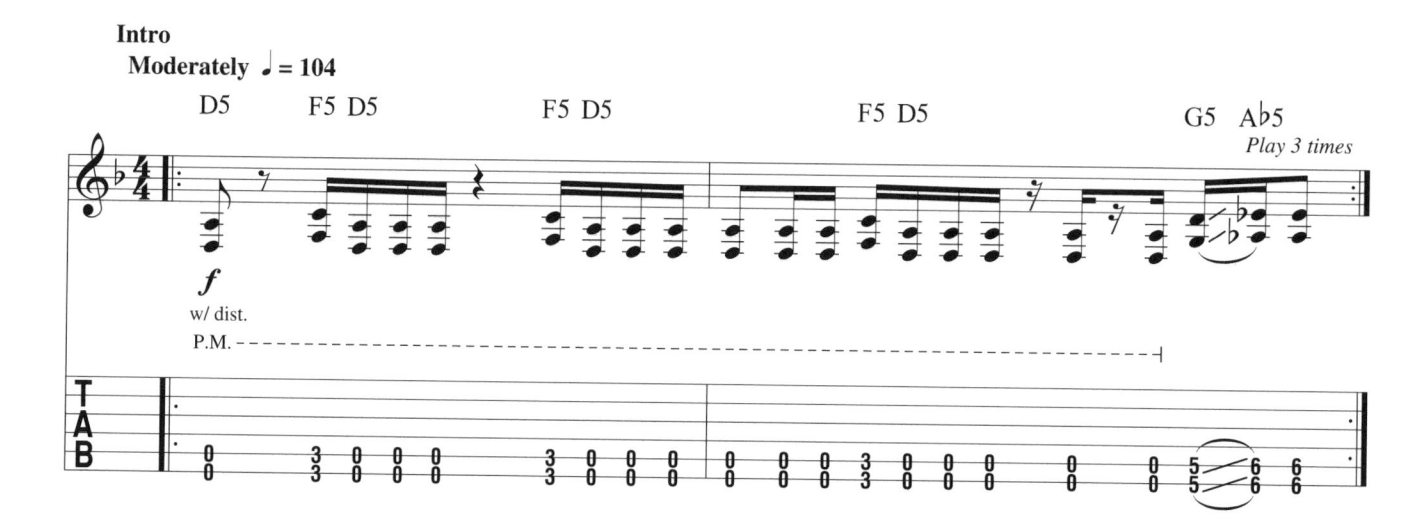

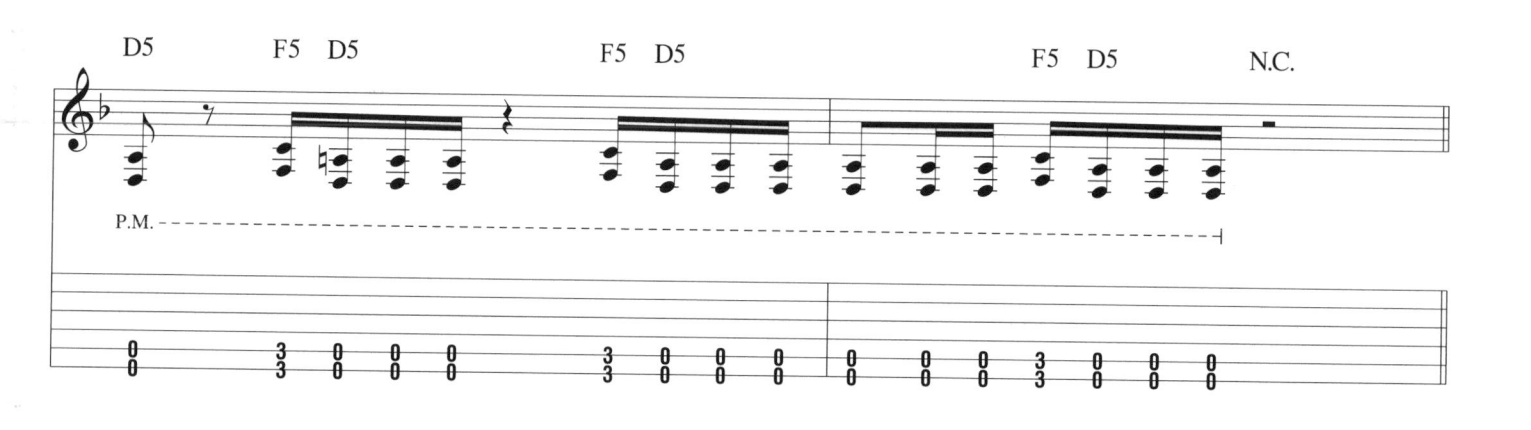

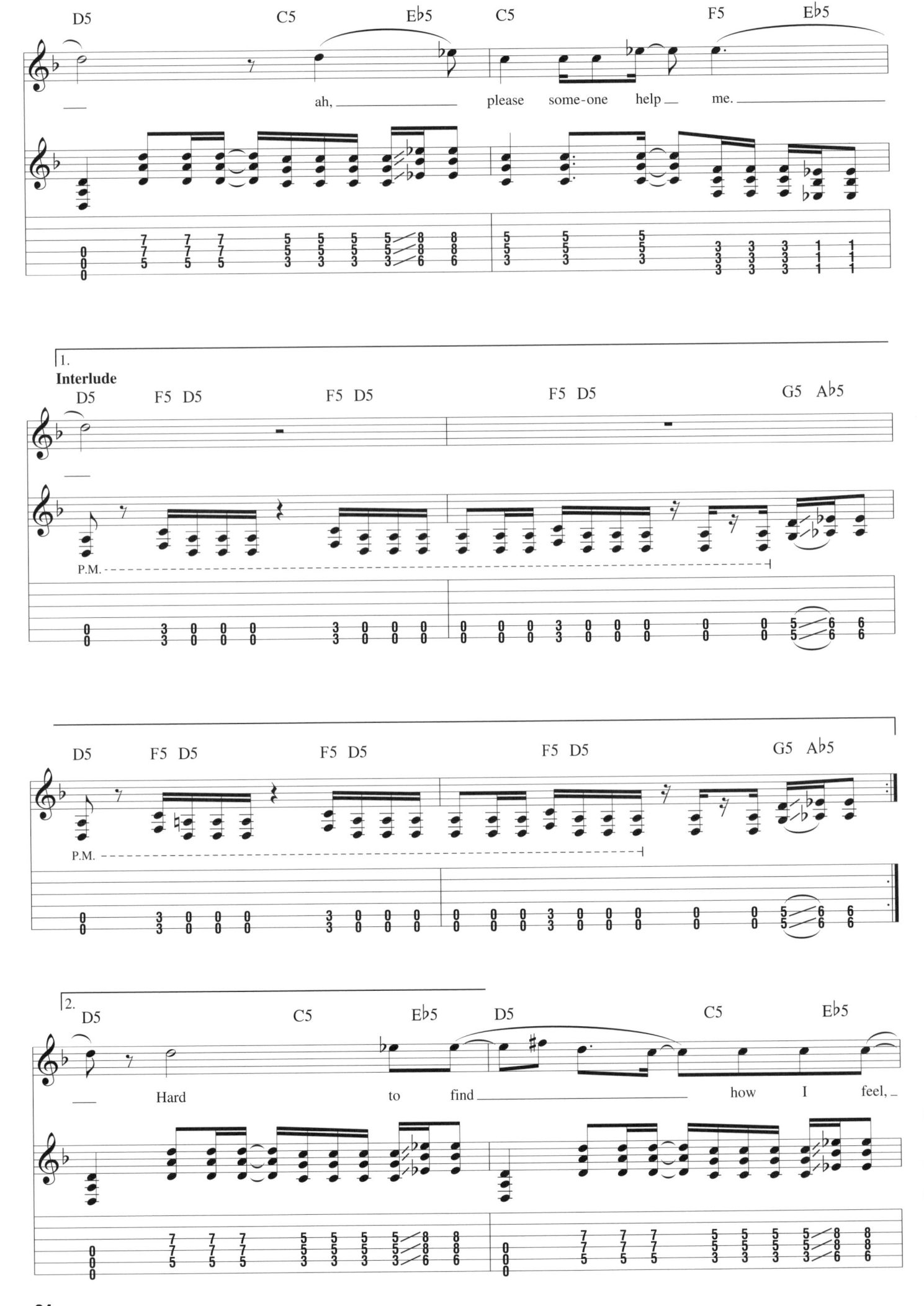

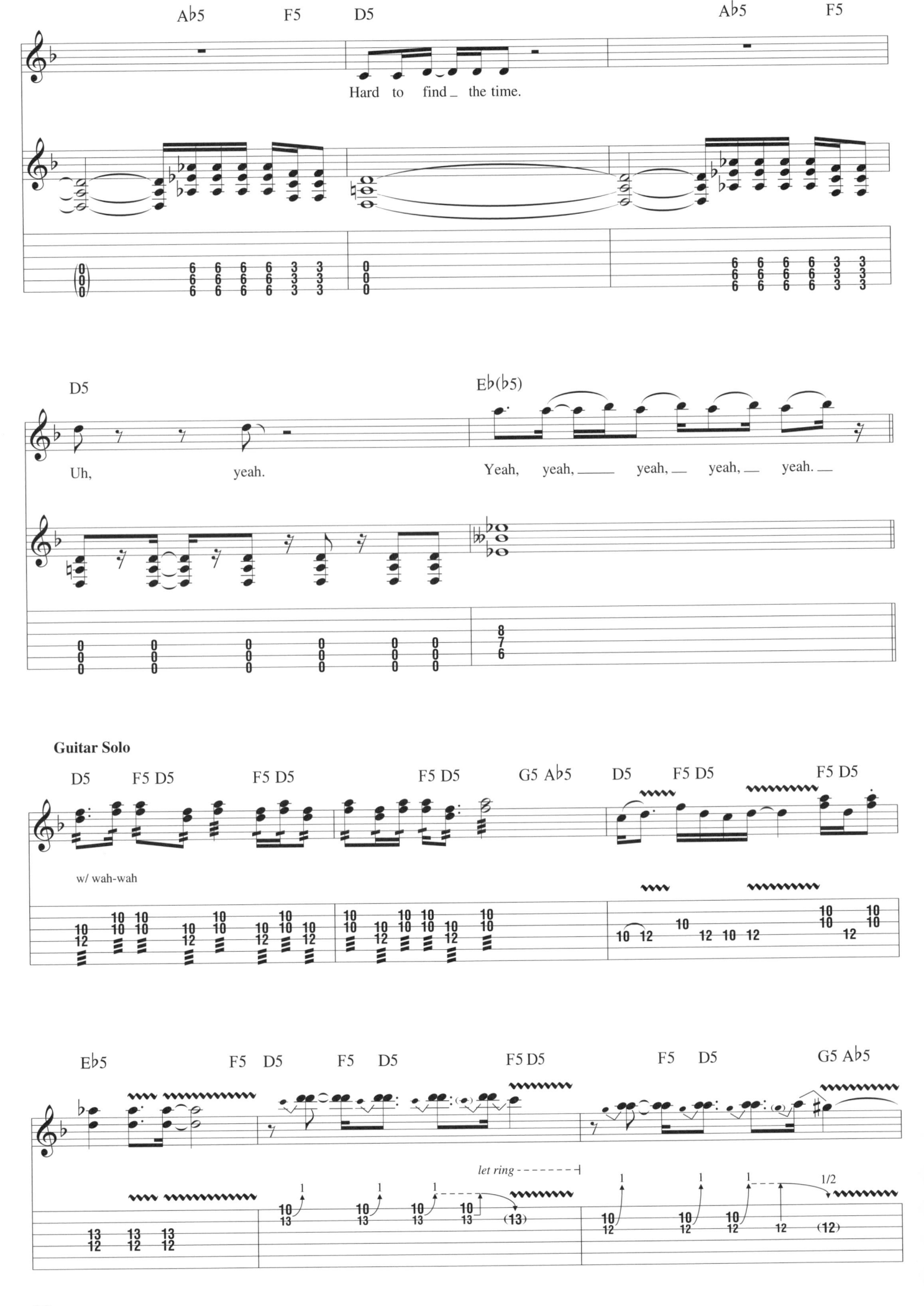

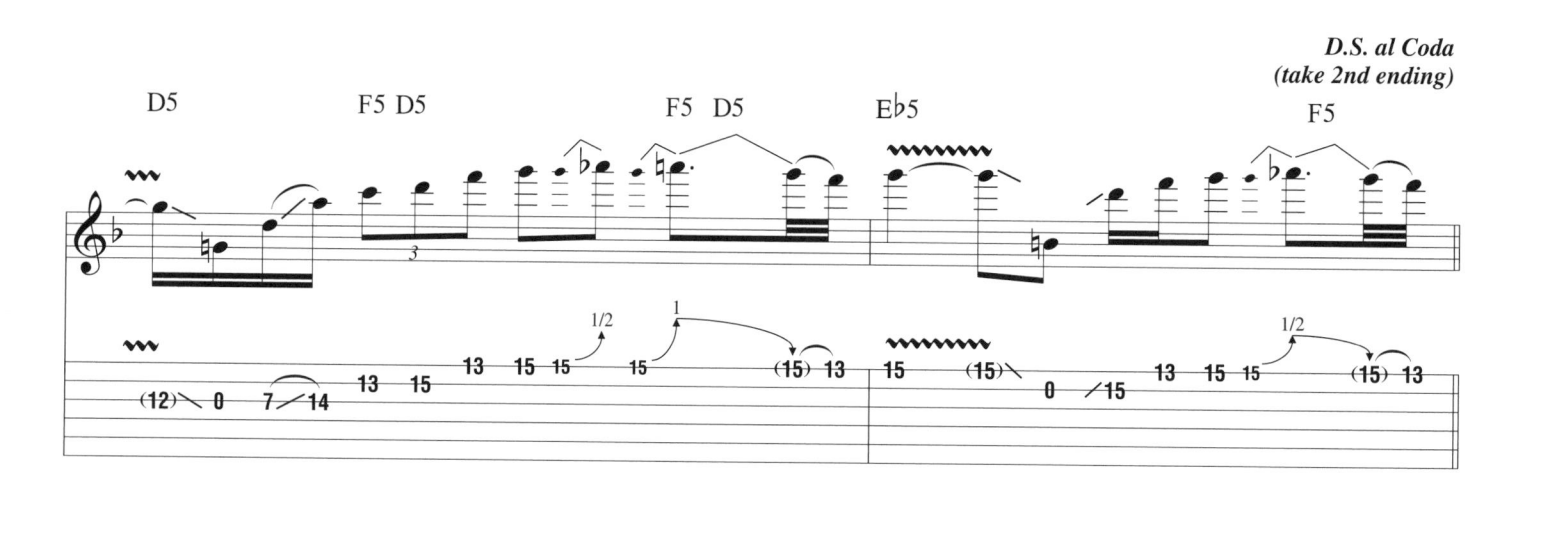

Coda

Outro

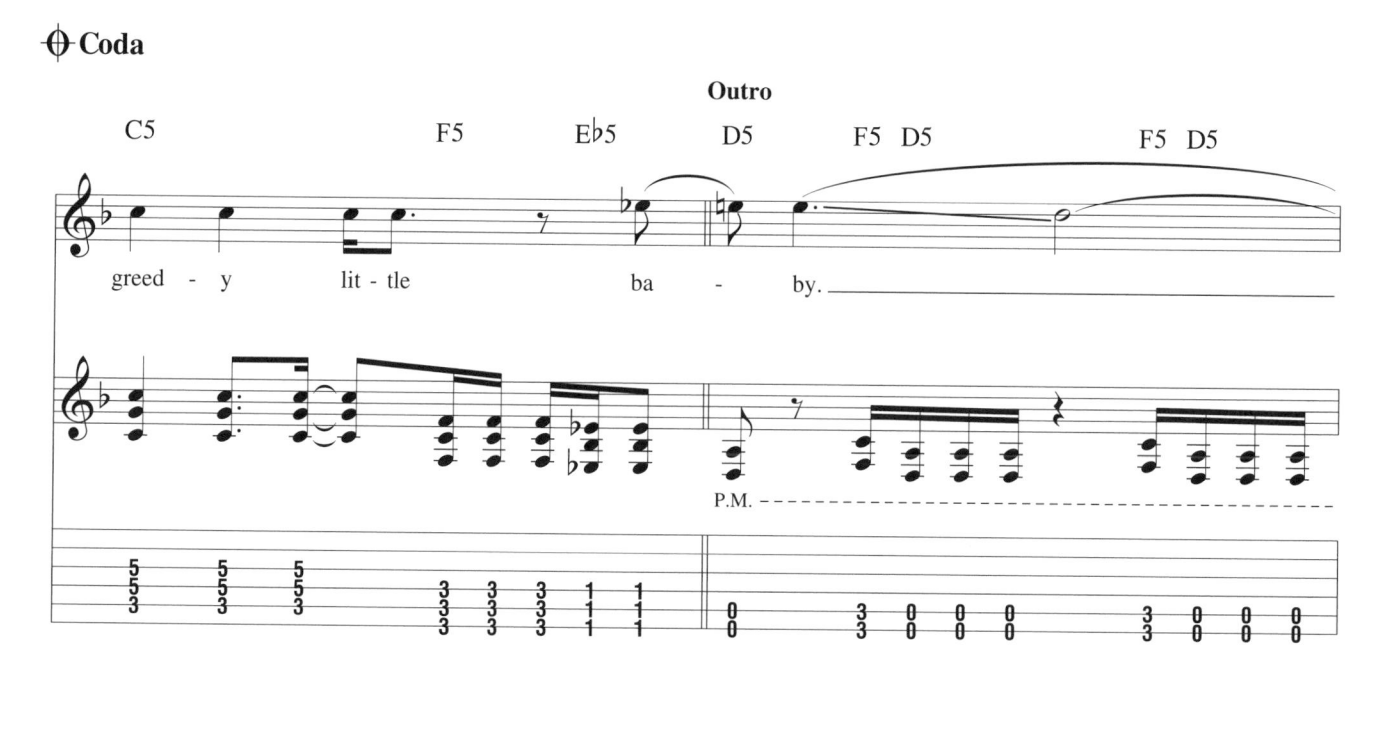

greed - y   lit - tle   ba -   by. ____

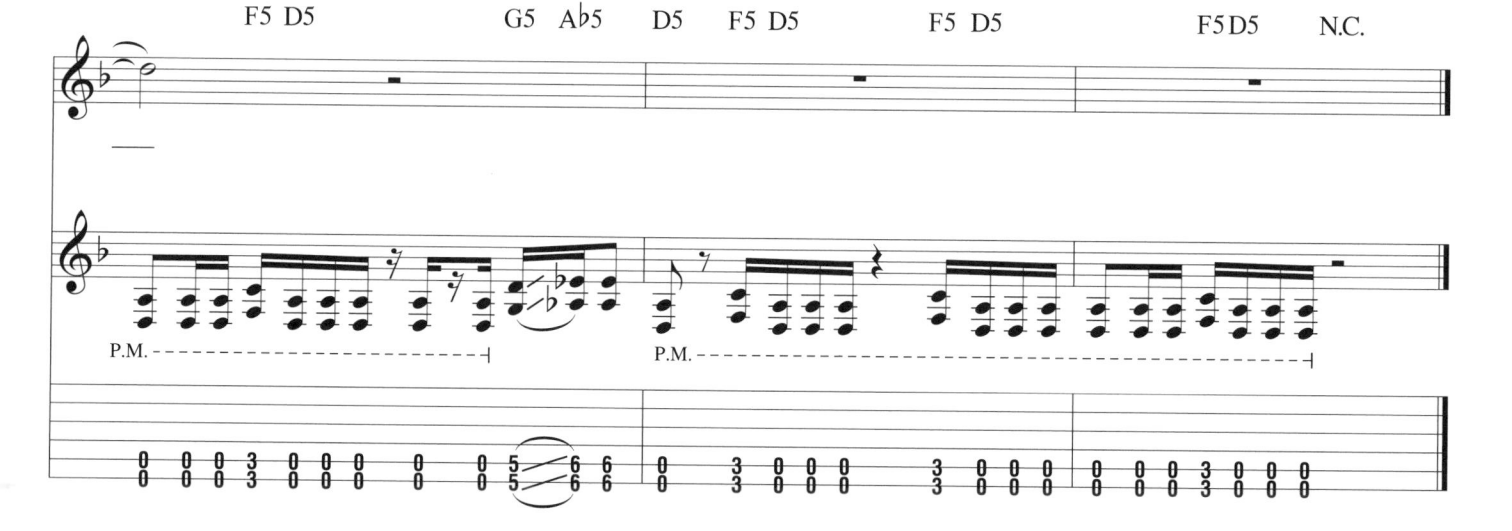

Additional Lyrics

2. I knew when an angel whispered into my ear,
   "You gotta get him away, yeah."
   Hey, little bitch, be glad you fin'ly walked away,
   Or you may have not lived another day.

I Stand Alone

Words and Music by Sully Erna

Drop D tuning, down 1 step:
(low to high) C-G-C-F-A-D

Intro

Moderately slow ♩ = 84

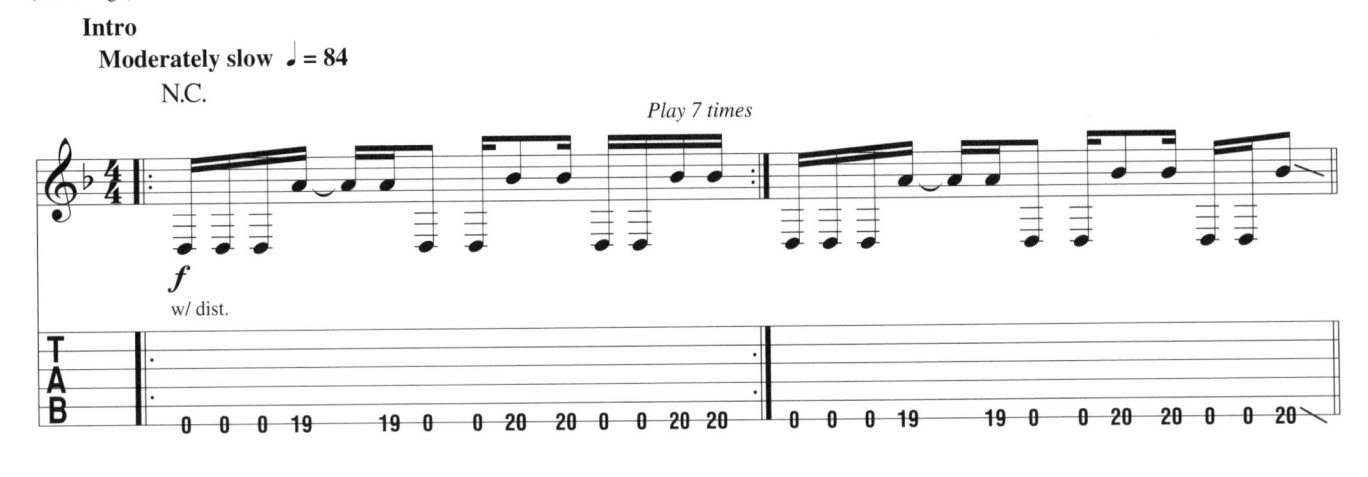

1. I've told ____ you this once be - fore, ____ can't con - trol me.
2. *See additional lyrics*

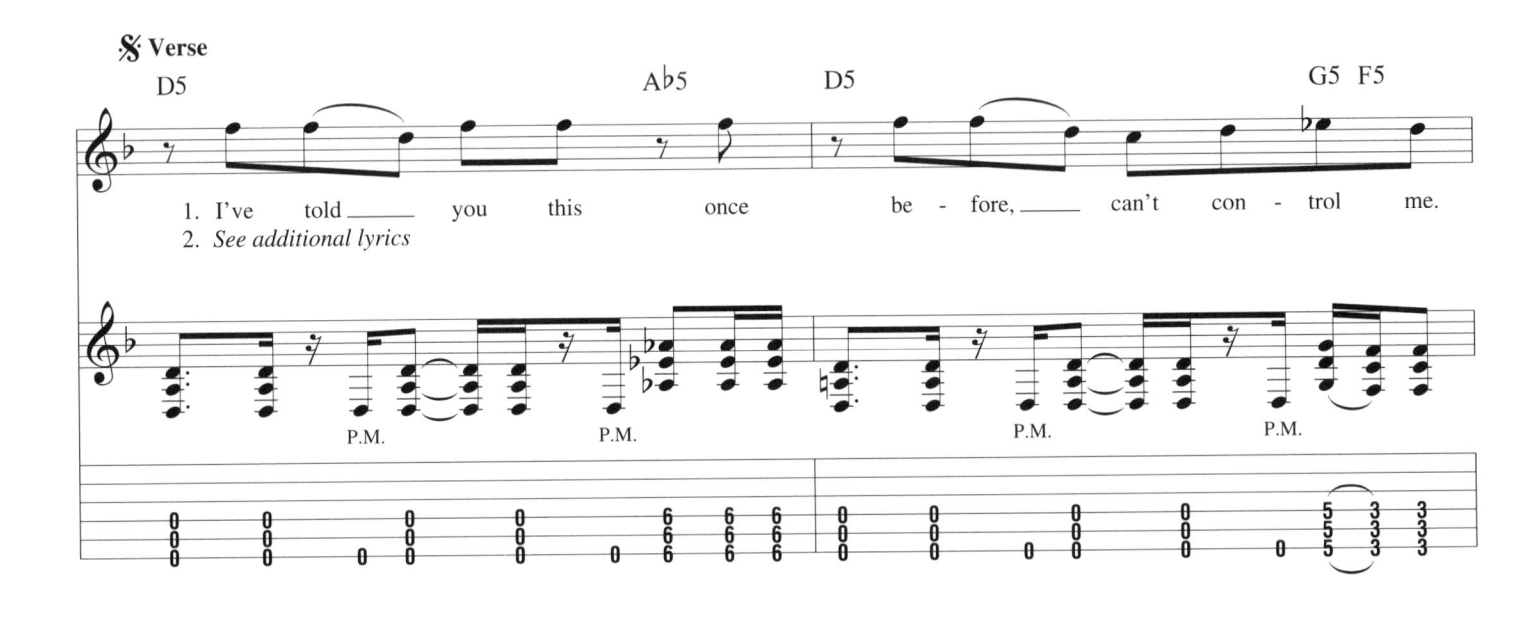

If you ____ try to ____ take me down you're gon - na break.

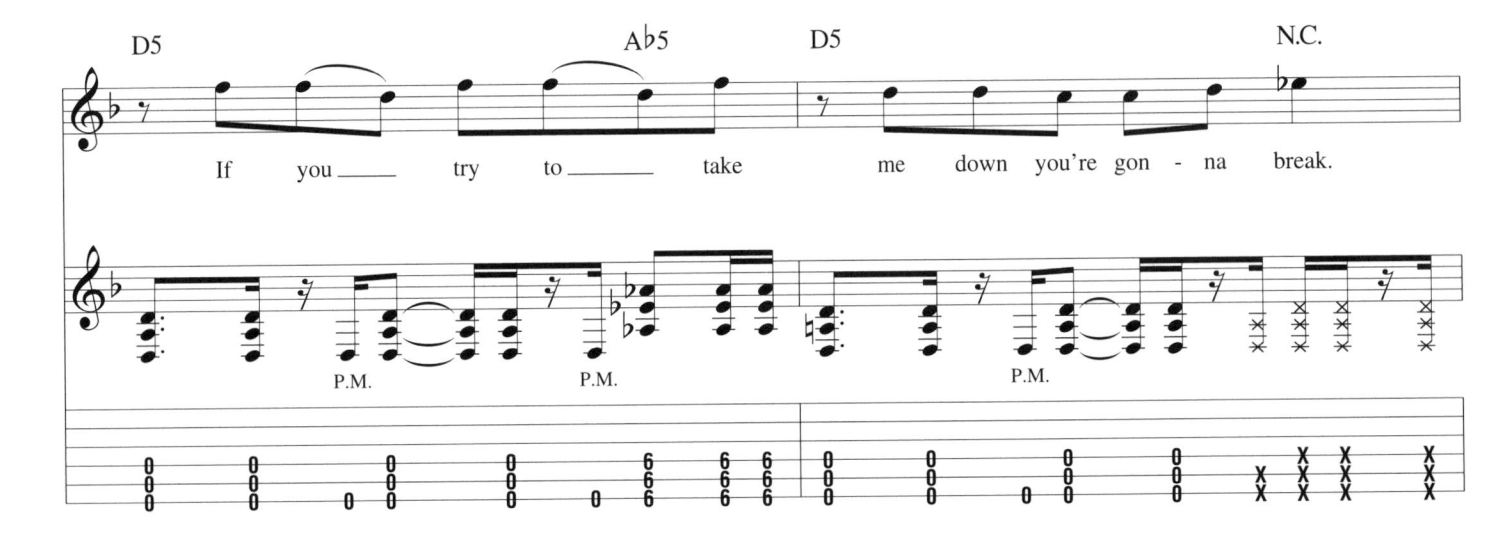

D5   Ab5   Ab sus2 add6

talkbox off

Chorus

N.C.

I _____ stand a - lone ___ in - side. ___

I _____ stand a - lone. ___ Feel - ing __ your

G5   Bb5

sting down __ in - side me, I'm not __ dy - ing for it. __

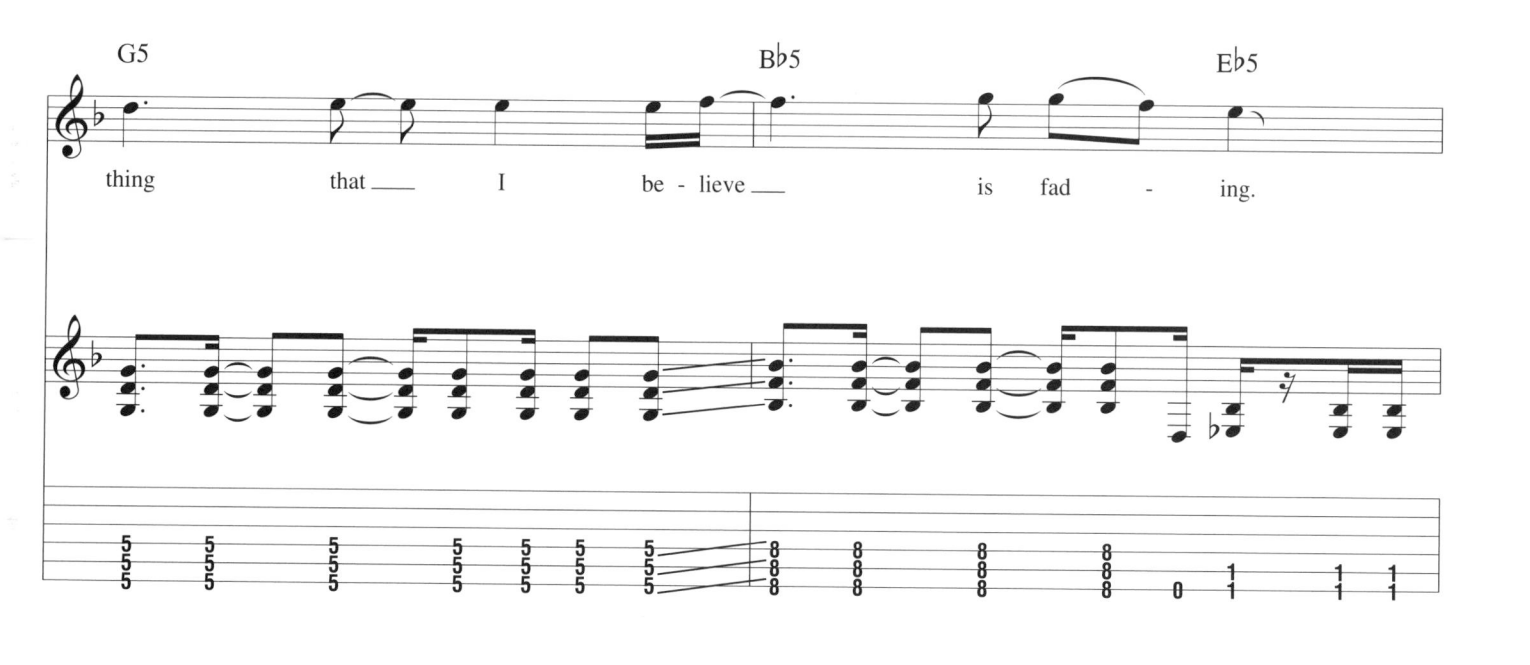

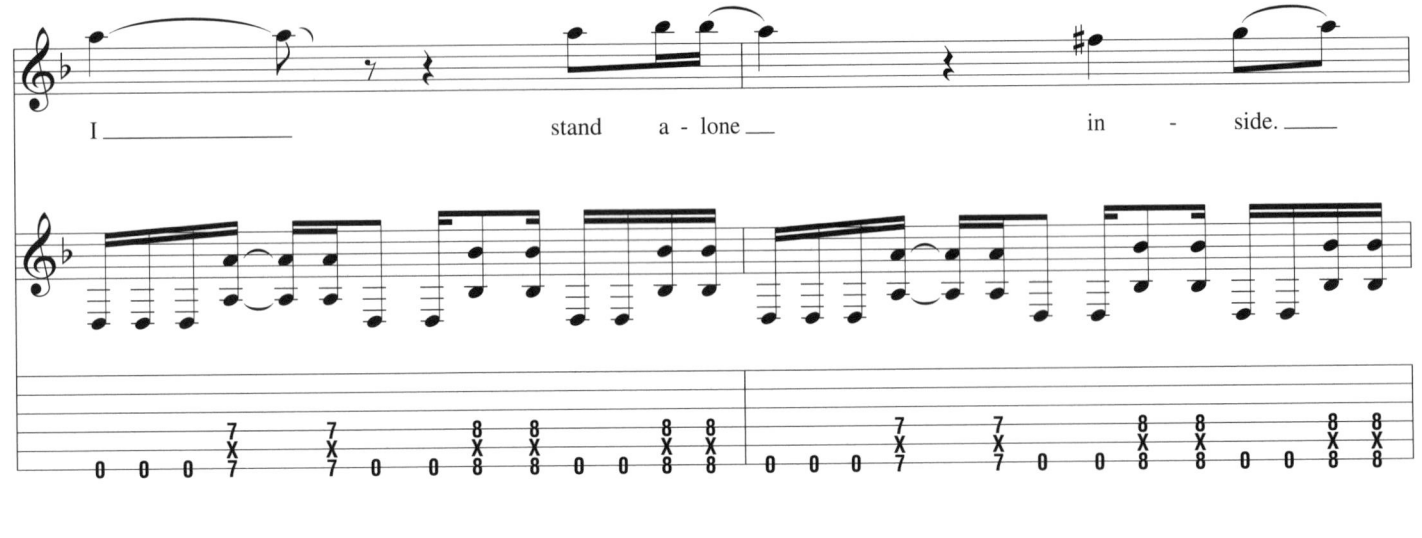

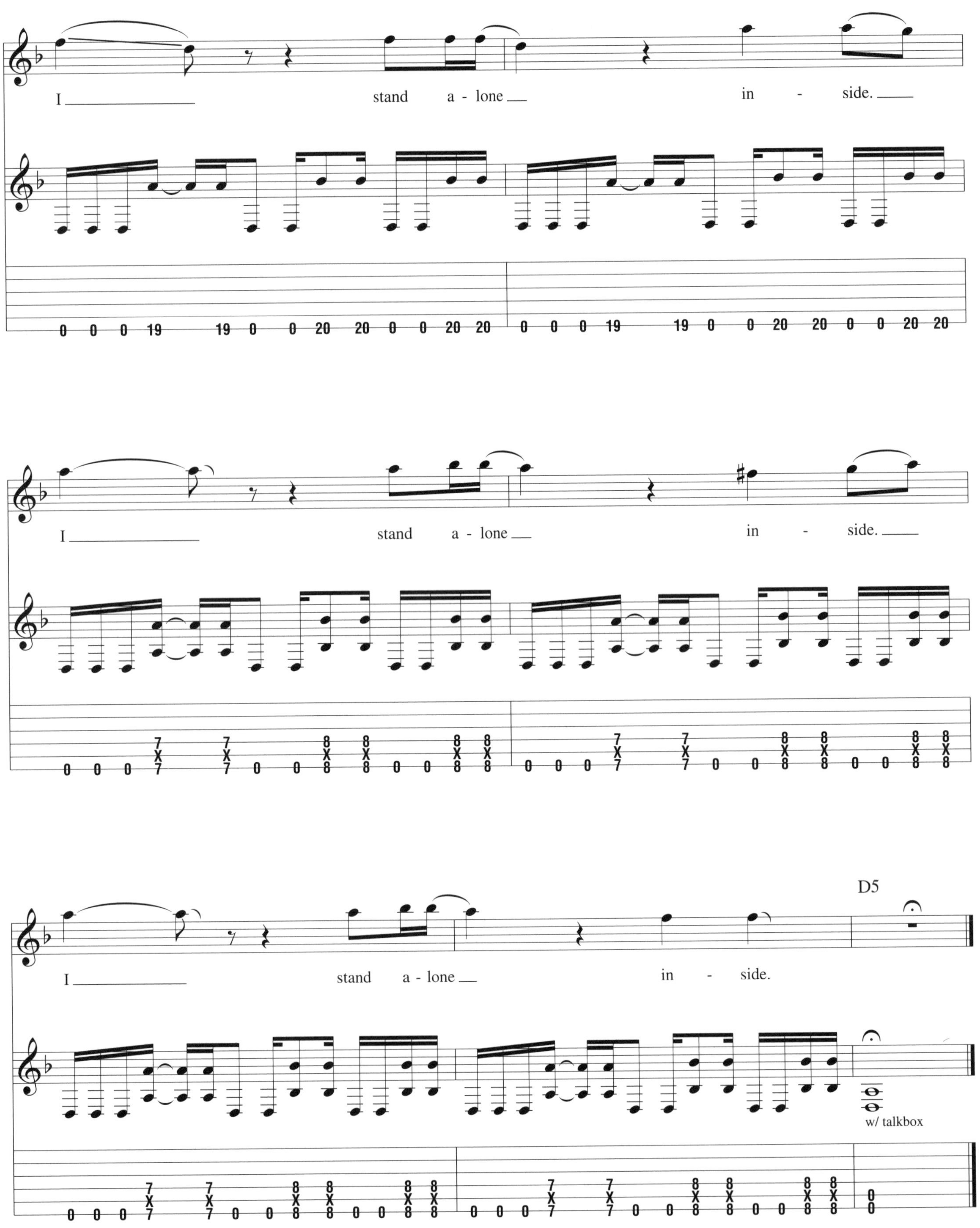

Additional Lyrics

2. You're always hiding behind you so-called goddess.
   So what? You don't think that we can see your face?
   Resurrected back before the final falling.
   And I'll never rest until I can make my own way.
   I'm not afraid of fading.

Running Blind

Words and Music by Sully Erna

Tune down 1/2 step:
(low to high) Eb-Ab-Db-Gb-Bb-Eb

Intro
Slowly ♩ = 66

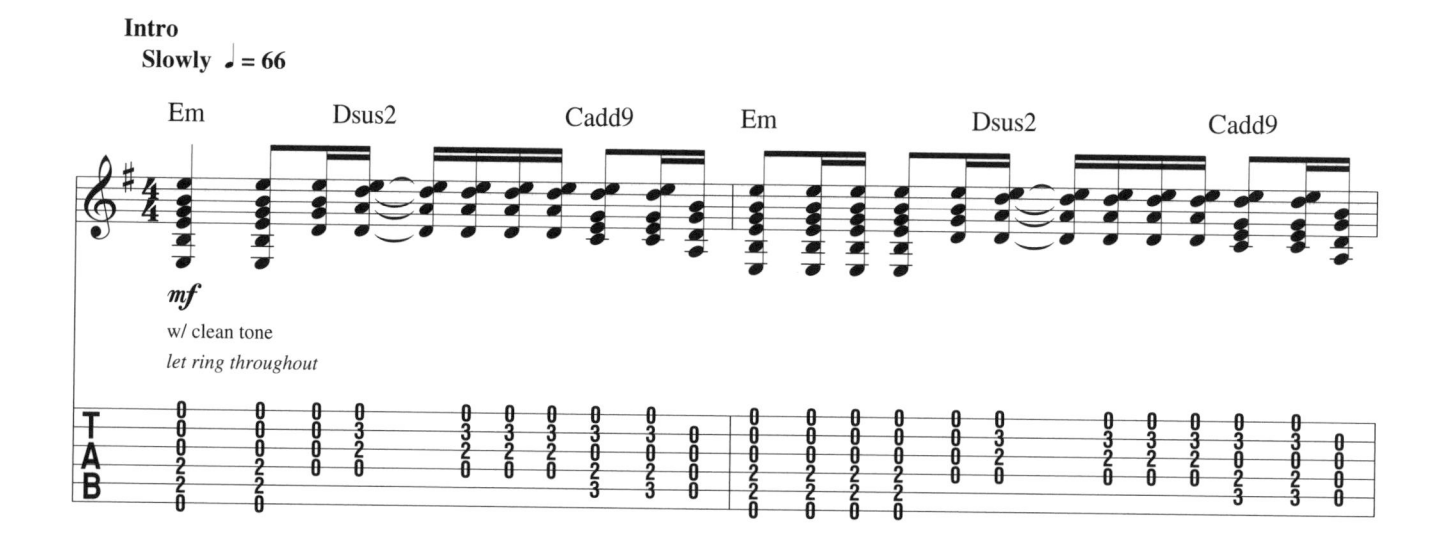

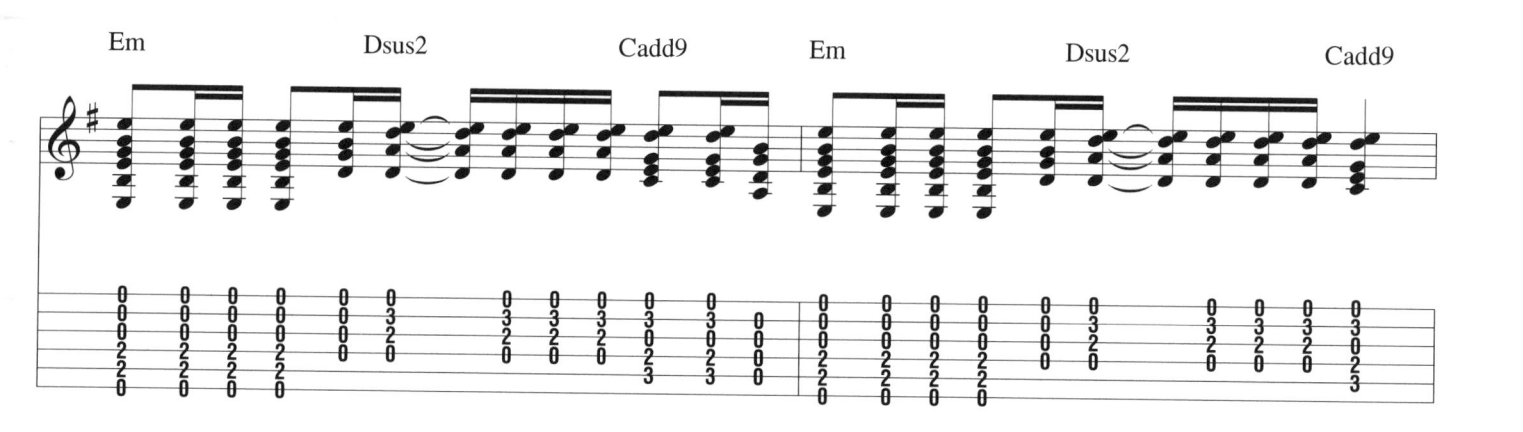

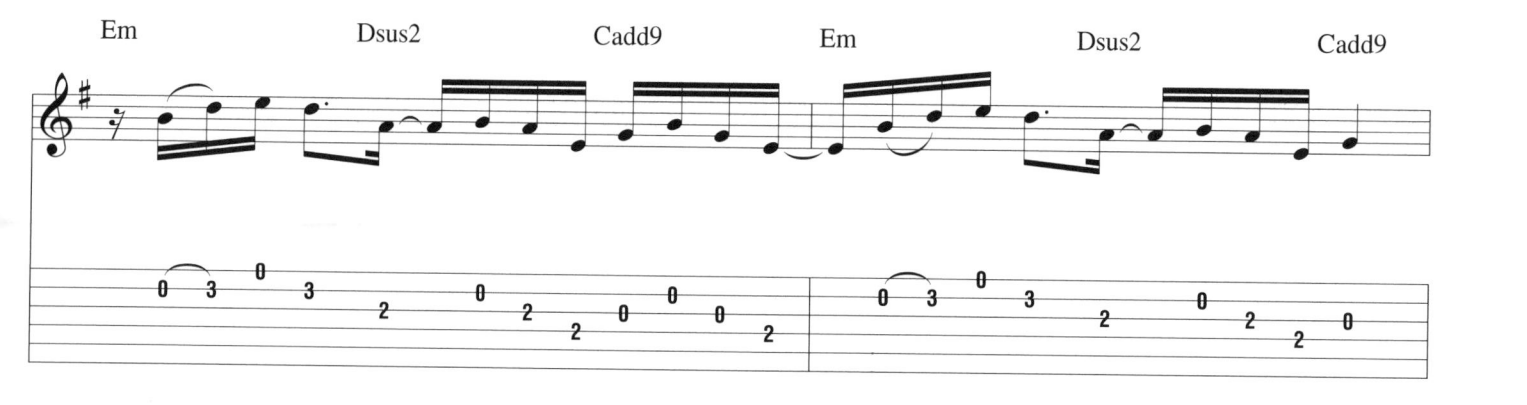

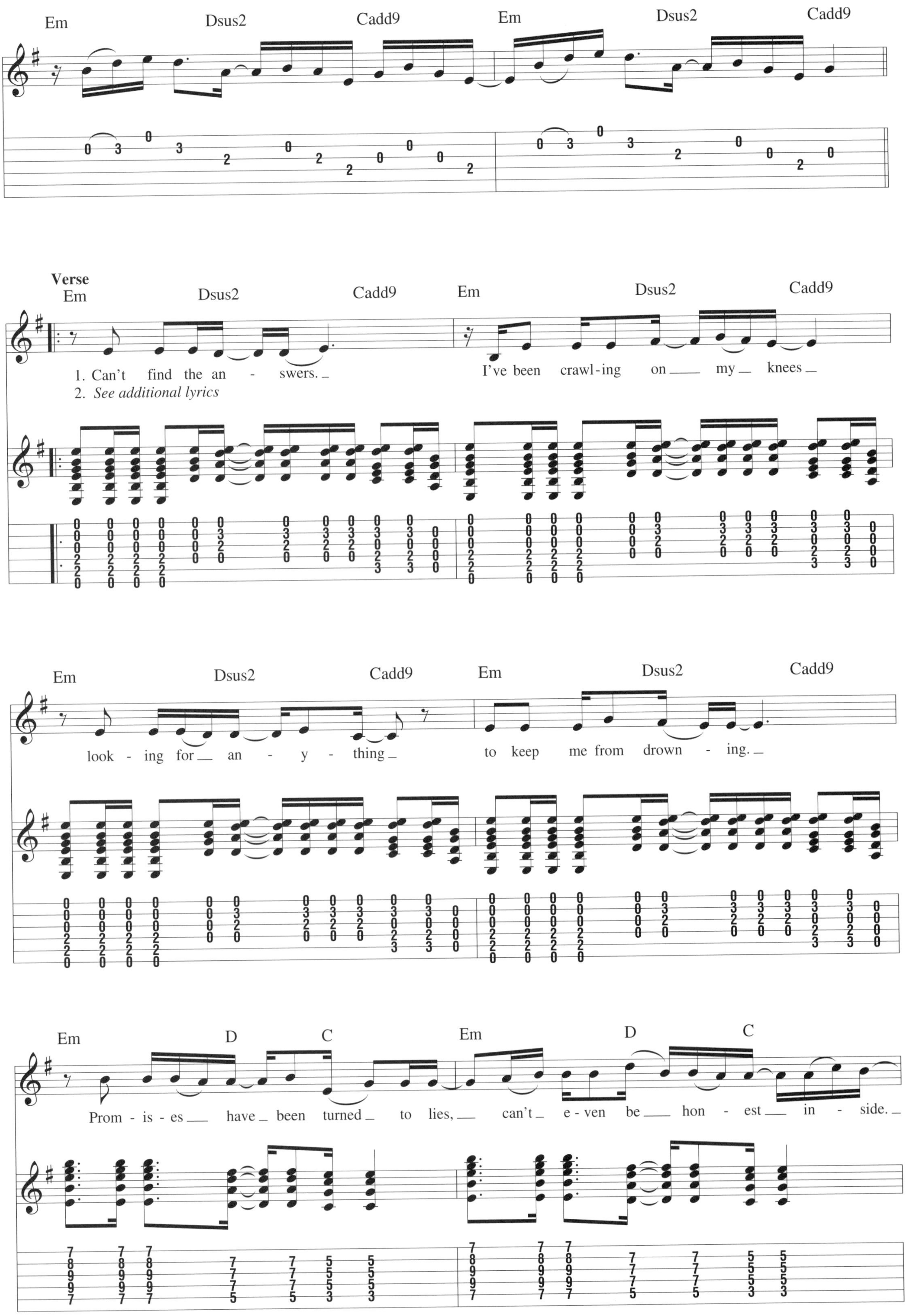

Em | Dsus2 | Cadd9 | Em | Dsus2 | Cadd9

Verse

Em | Dsus2 | Cadd9 | Em | Dsus2 | Cadd9

1. Can't find the an - swers. _ I've been crawl-ing on __ my __ knees __
2. *See additional lyrics*

Em | Dsus2 | Cadd9 | Em | Dsus2 | Cadd9

look - ing for __ an - y - thing __ to keep me from drown - ing. _

Em | D | C | Em | D | C

Prom - is - es __ have _ been turned _ to lies, _ can't _ e - ven be hon - est __ in - side.

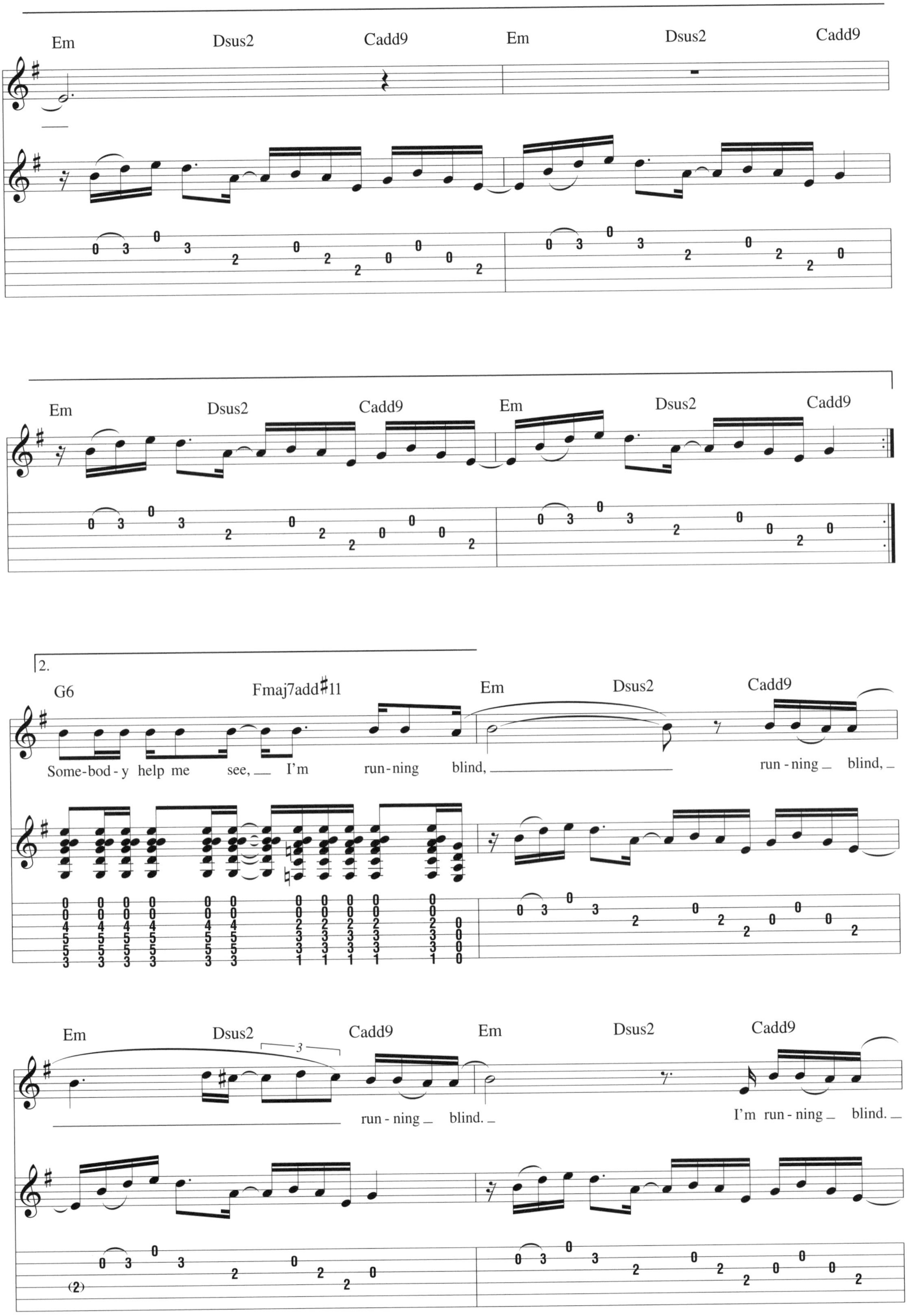
Em Dsus2 Cadd9 Em Dsus2 Cadd9
Em Dsus2 Cadd9 Em Dsus2 Cadd9
2.
G6 Fmaj7add♯11 Em Dsus2 Cadd9
Some-bod-y help me see, I'm run-ning blind, run-ning blind,
Em Dsus2 Cadd9 Em Dsus2 Cadd9
run-ning blind. I'm run-ning blind.

Guitar Solo

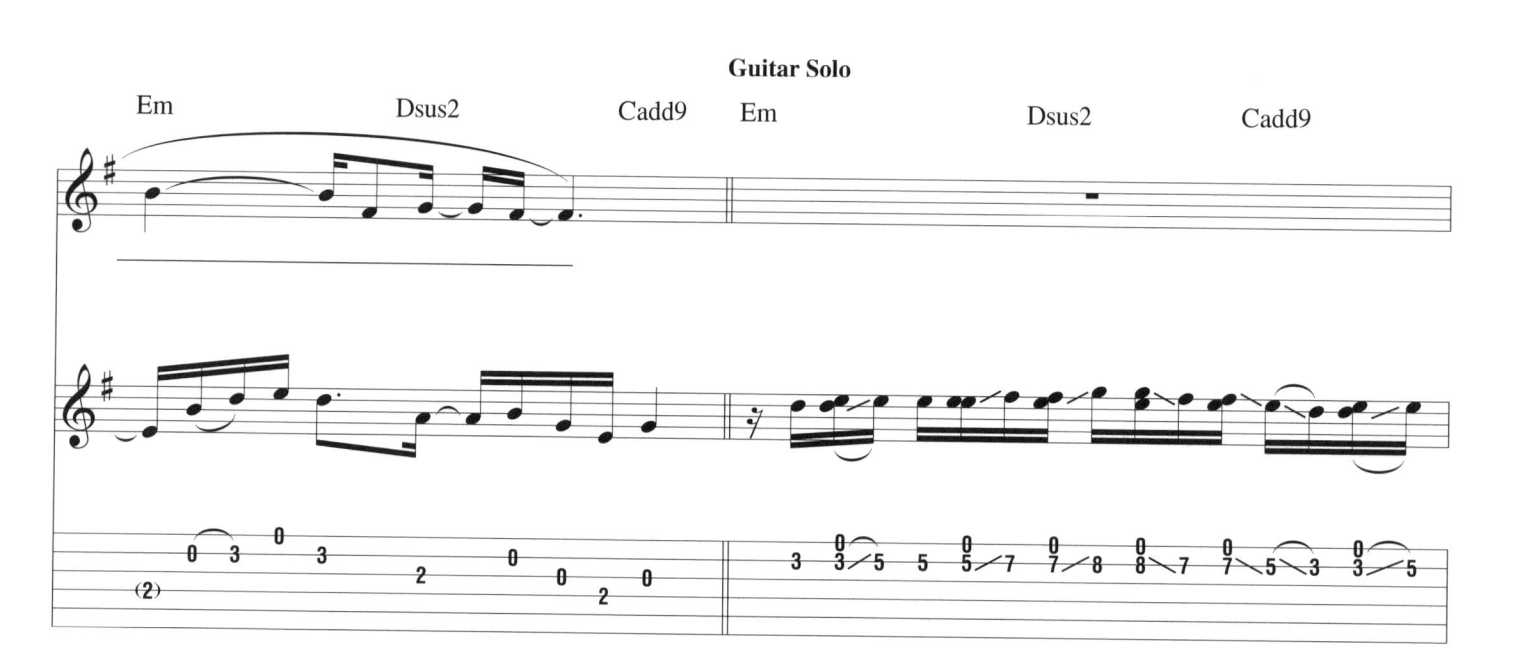

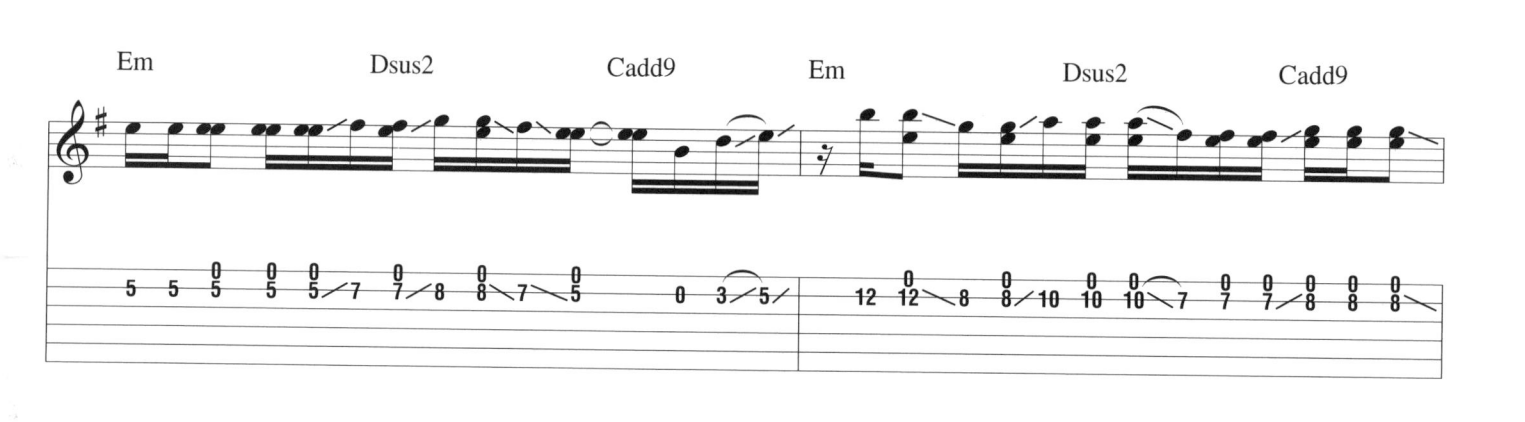

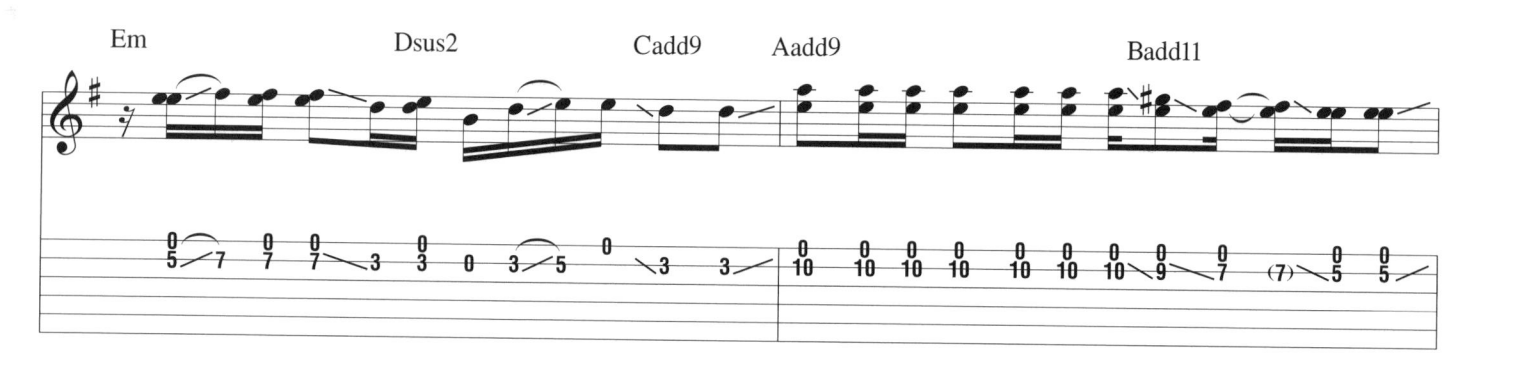

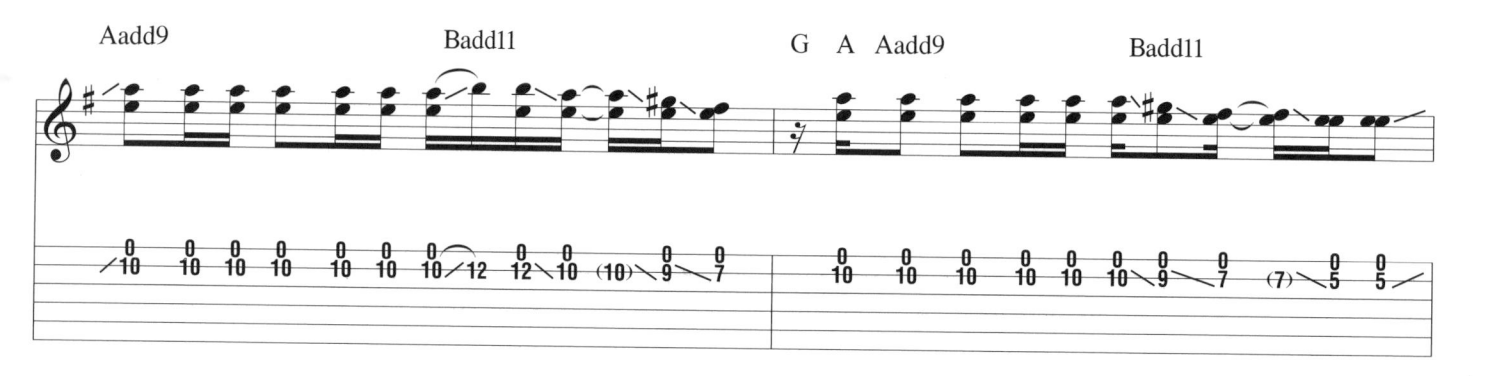

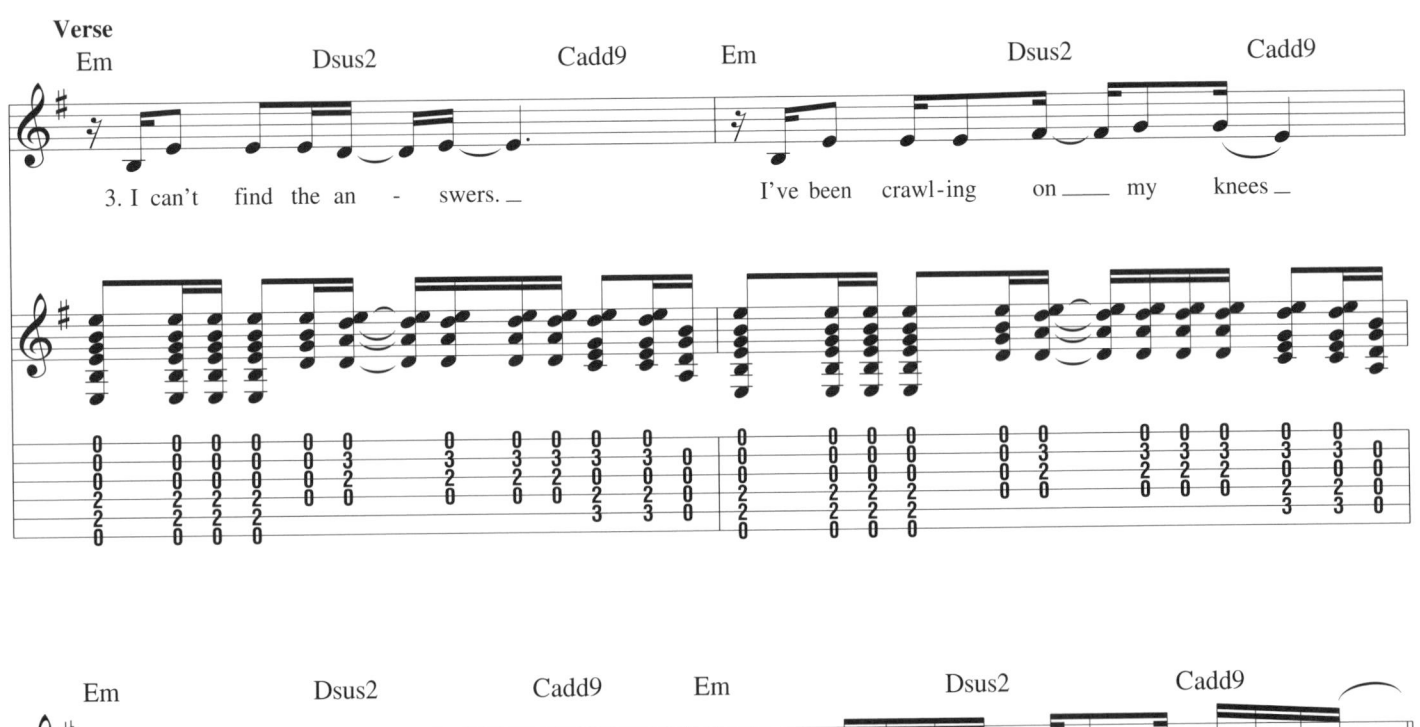

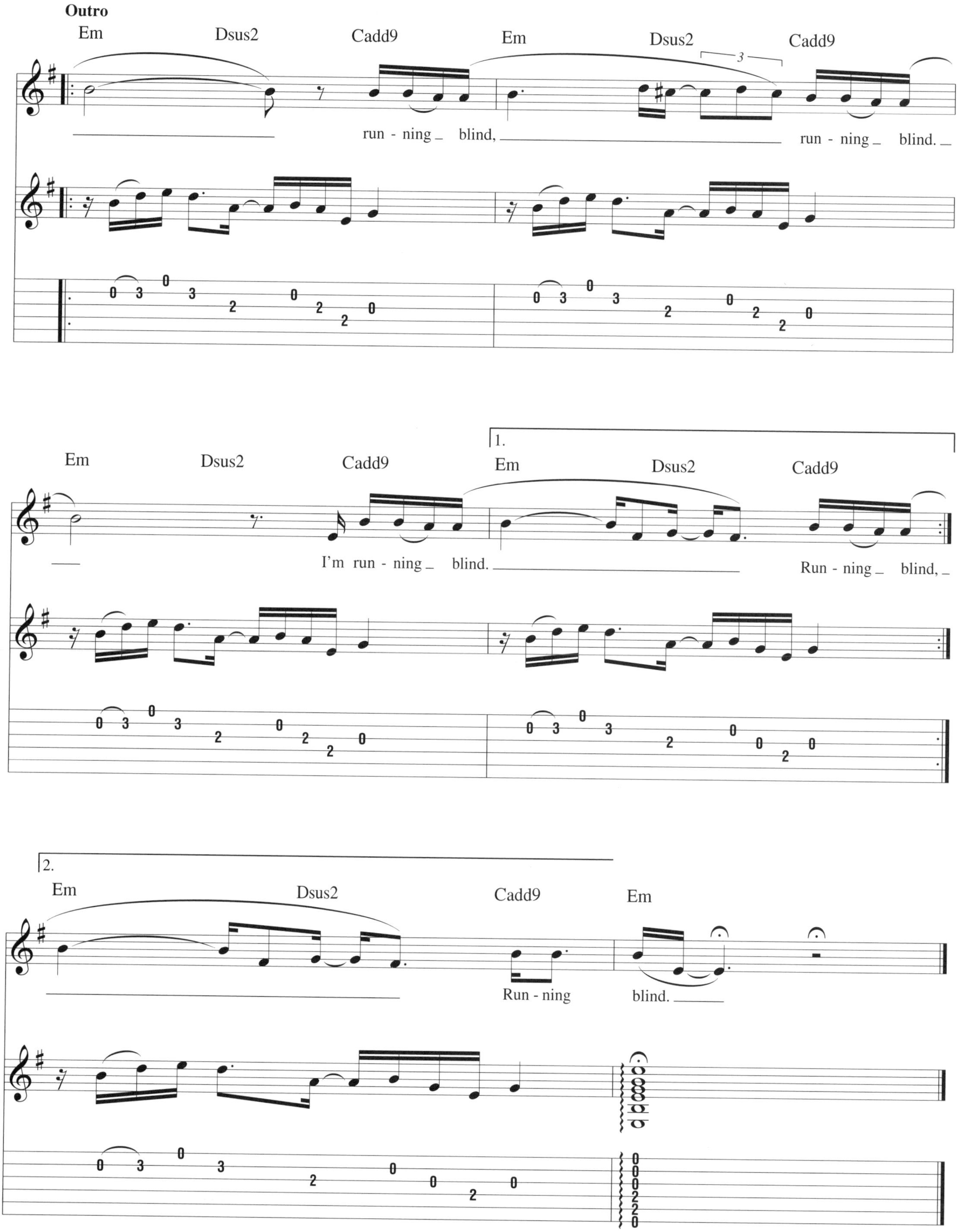

Outro
Em
Dsus2
Cadd9
Em
Dsus2
3
Cadd9
run - ning blind,
run - ning blind.
Em
Dsus2
Cadd9
1.
Em
Dsus2
Cadd9
I'm run - ning blind.
Run - ning blind,
2.
Em
Dsus2
Cadd9
Em
Run - ning
blind.

Additional Lyrics

2. Searching for nothing, wondering if I'll change.
I'm trying ev'rything, but ev'rything still stays the same.
I thought if I showed you I could fly, wouldn't need anyone by my side.
Now I'm crawling backward, with broken wings I know I'll die.

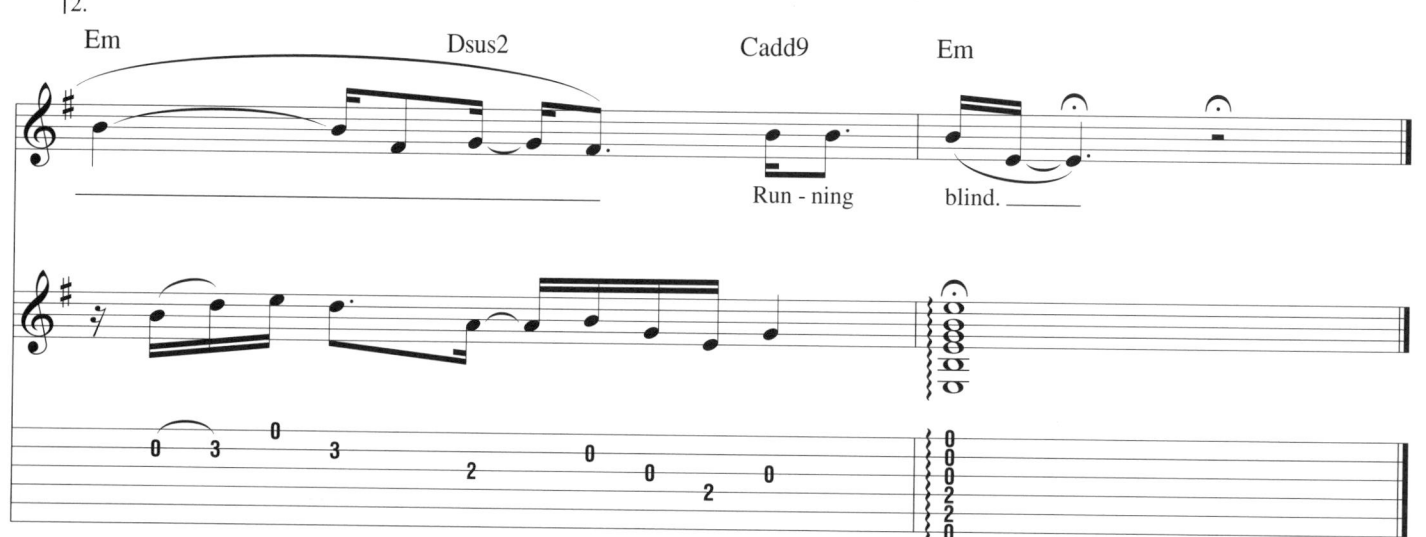

Keep Away

Words and Music by Sully Erna

Drop D tuning:
(low to high) D-A-D-G-B-D

Moderately ♩ = 98

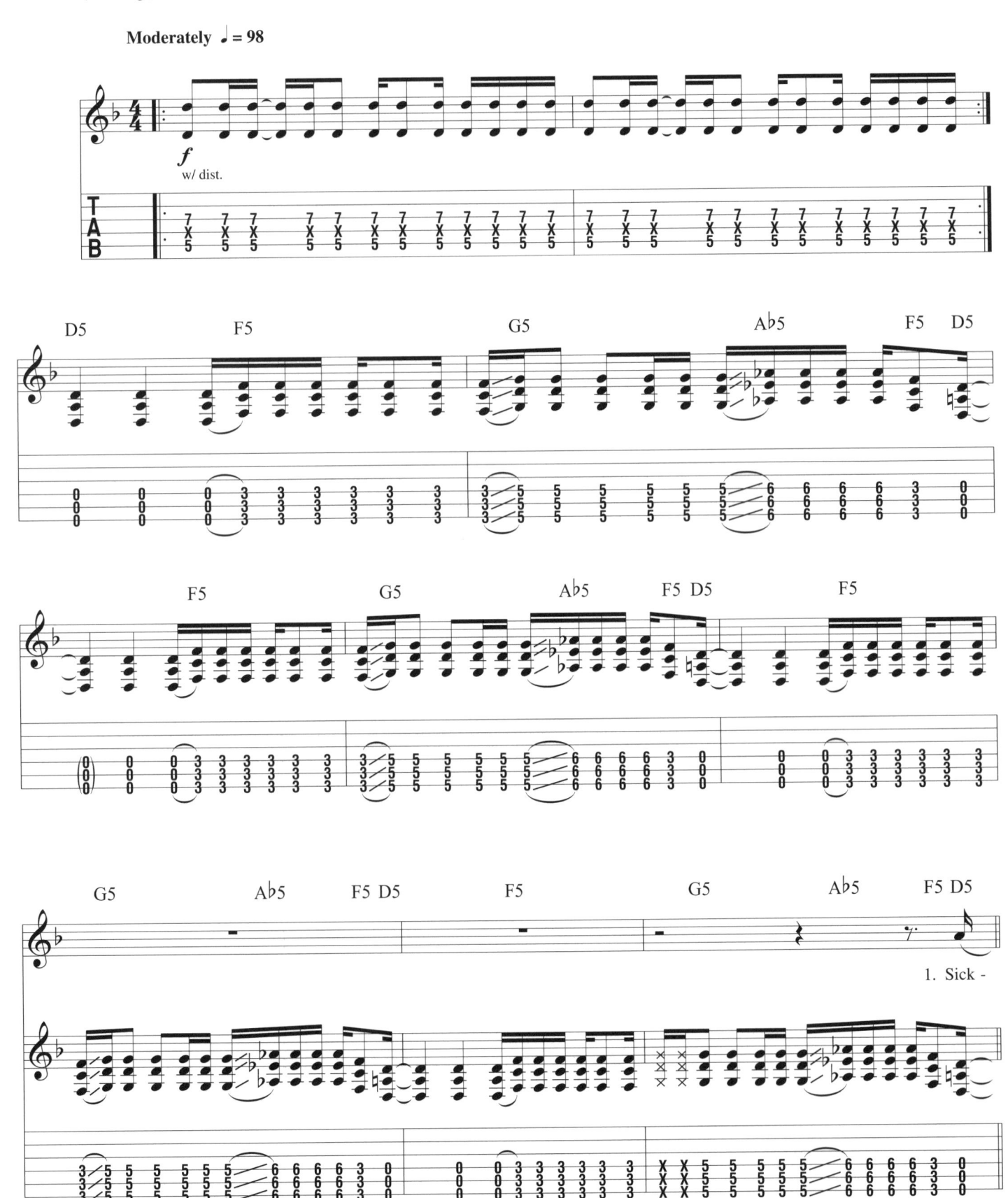

1. Sick -

Verse
3rd time, substitute Fill 1
D5 F5 G5 Ab5 F5 D5
2. Stab me, uh, in my heart a - gain,
4., 5. See additional lyrics
F5 G5 Ab5 F5 D5
ah yeah. Drag
F5 G5 Ab5 F5 D5
me through your wast - ed life, are you for -

Fill 1

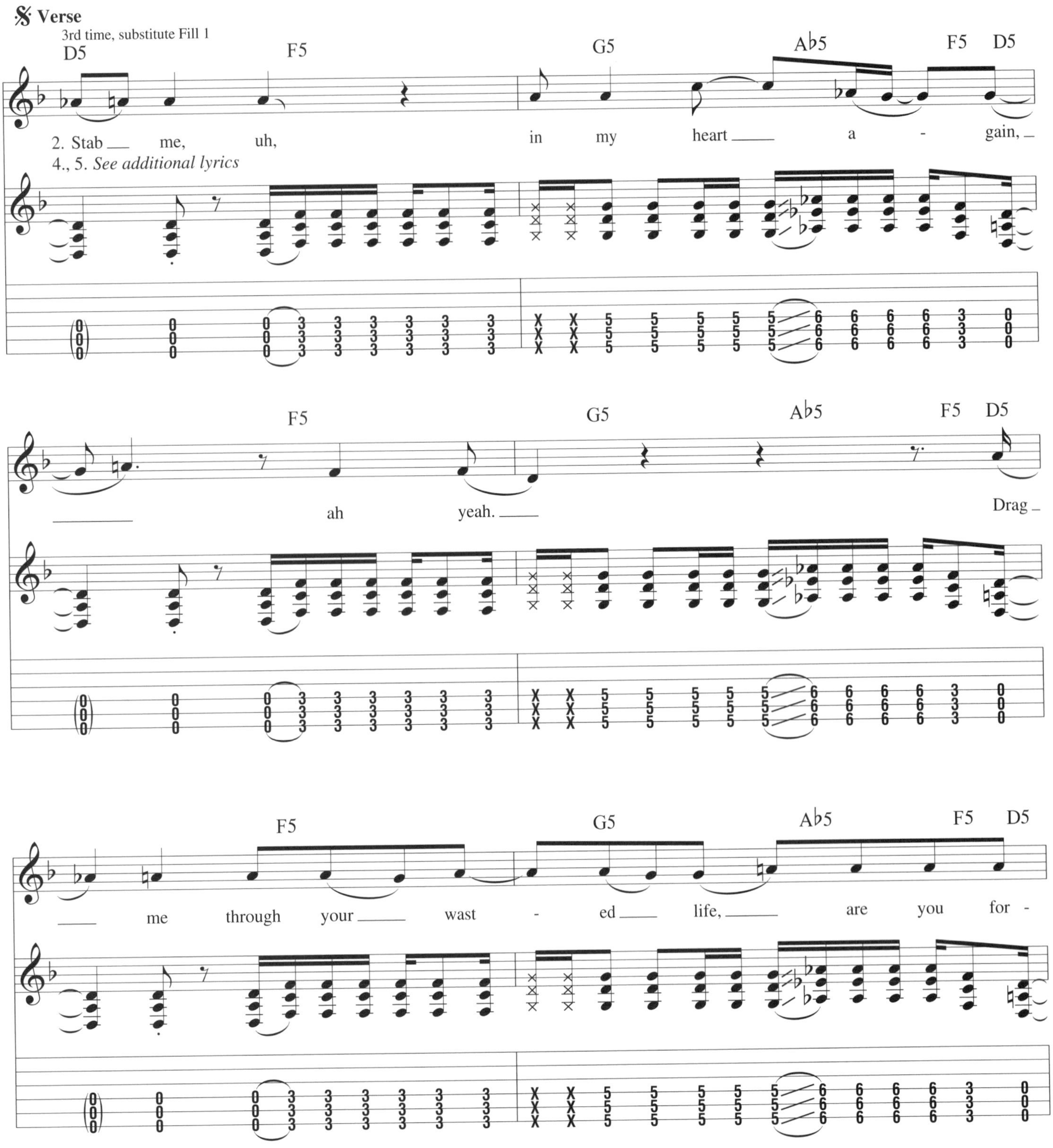

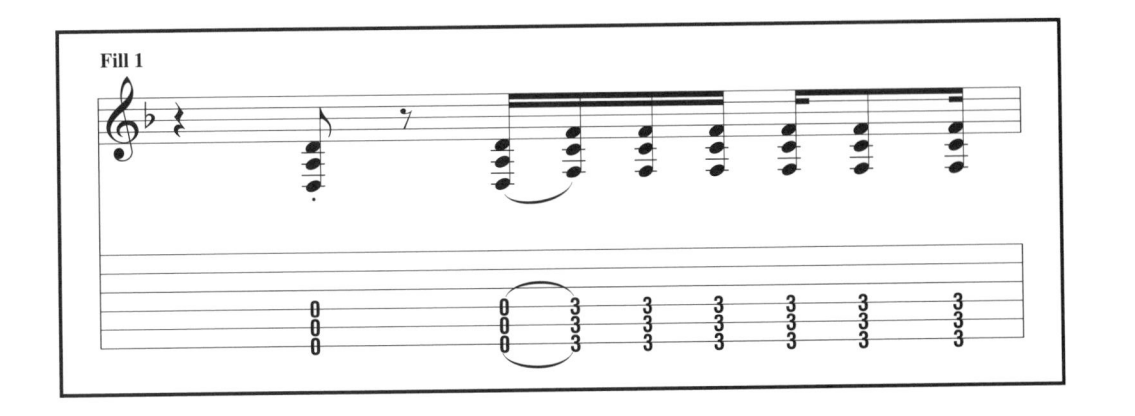

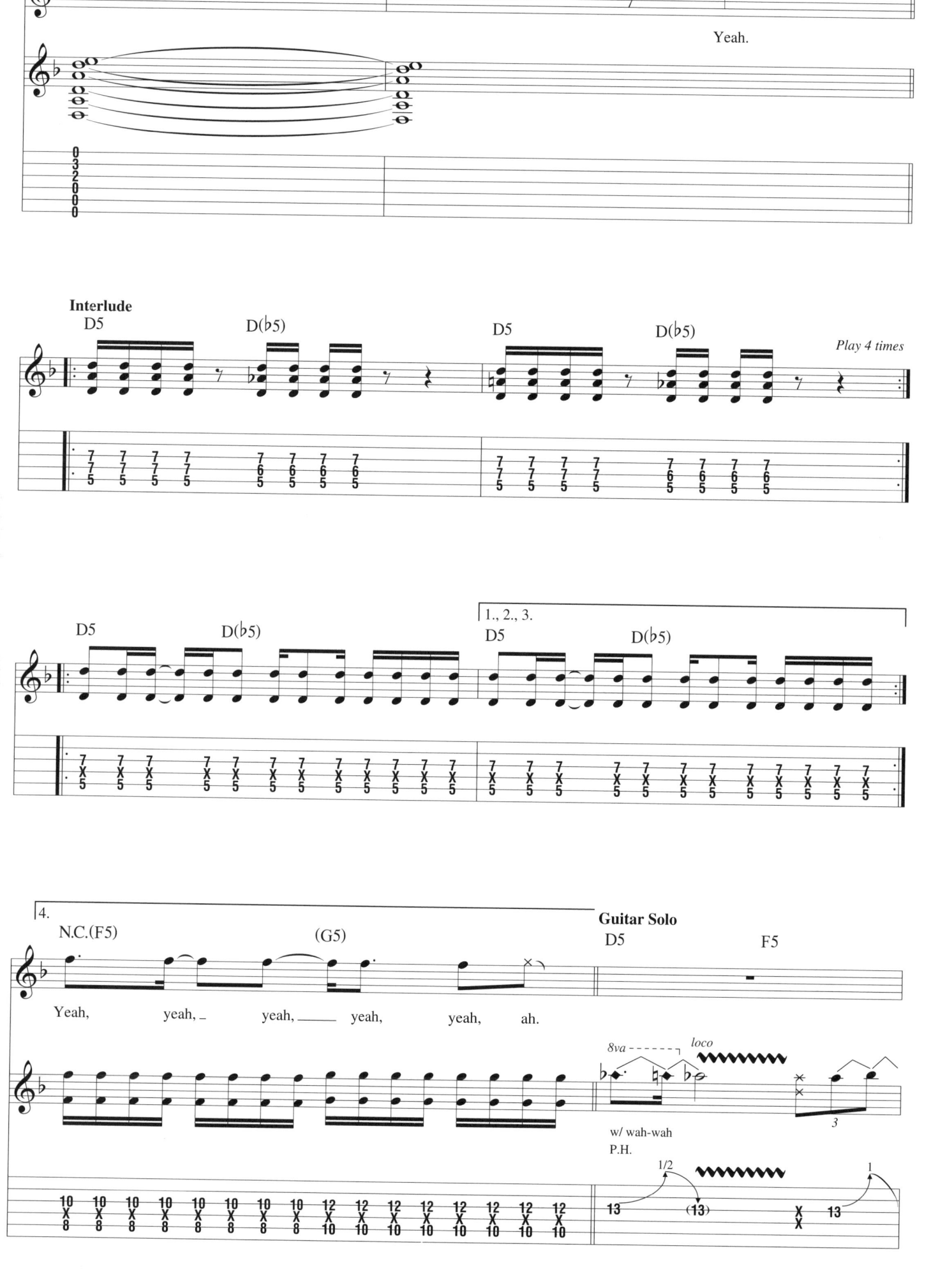

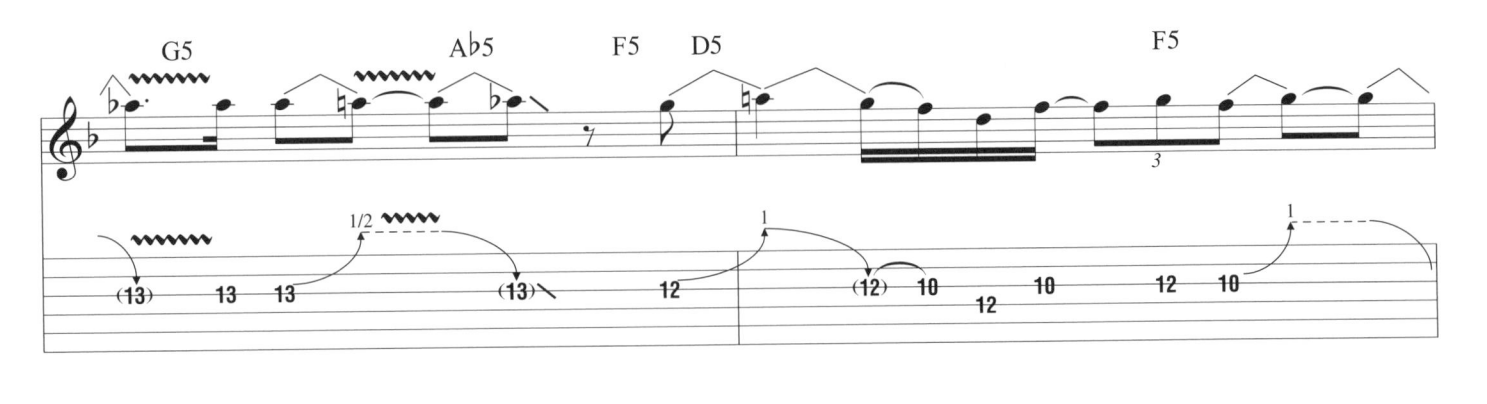

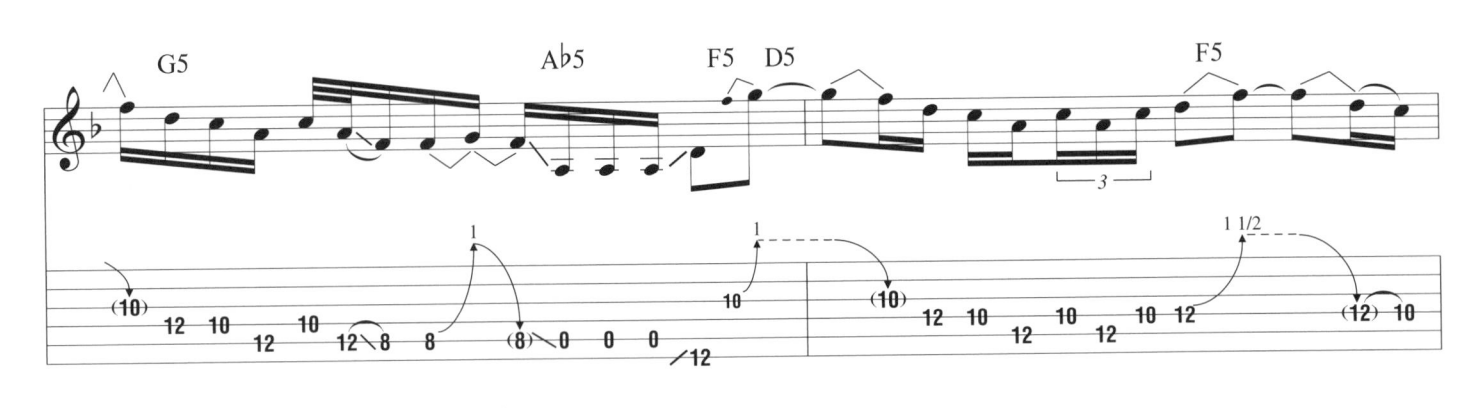

D.S. al Coda
(take 2nd ending)

Nev - er mis - un - der - stand ___ me. __

I, _____

Additional Lyrics

3. Twistin' ev'rything around that you say, yeah.
   Smack me in my mouth two hundred times ev'ry other day. Oh.

4. Rag me, uh, I don't hear you anymore, not yet.
   Find out what it means to me, I don't know who you are.
   Ah, ooh, oh, oh.

5. Draggin' on so lonely, aren't you tired, baby? Yeah.
   Breathing life into your lungs, are you immune to me?
   Ah, yeah, yeah, yeah, yeah.

Whatever

Words and Music by Sully Erna and Tony Rombola

Drop D tuning, down 1 step:
(low to high) C-G-C-F-A-D

Intro
Moderate Rock ♩ = 122

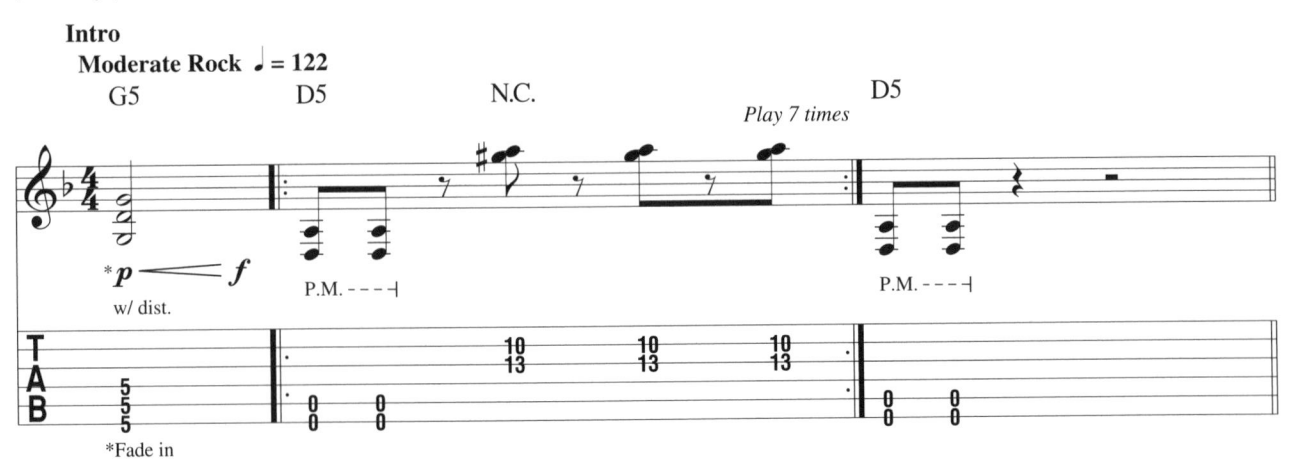

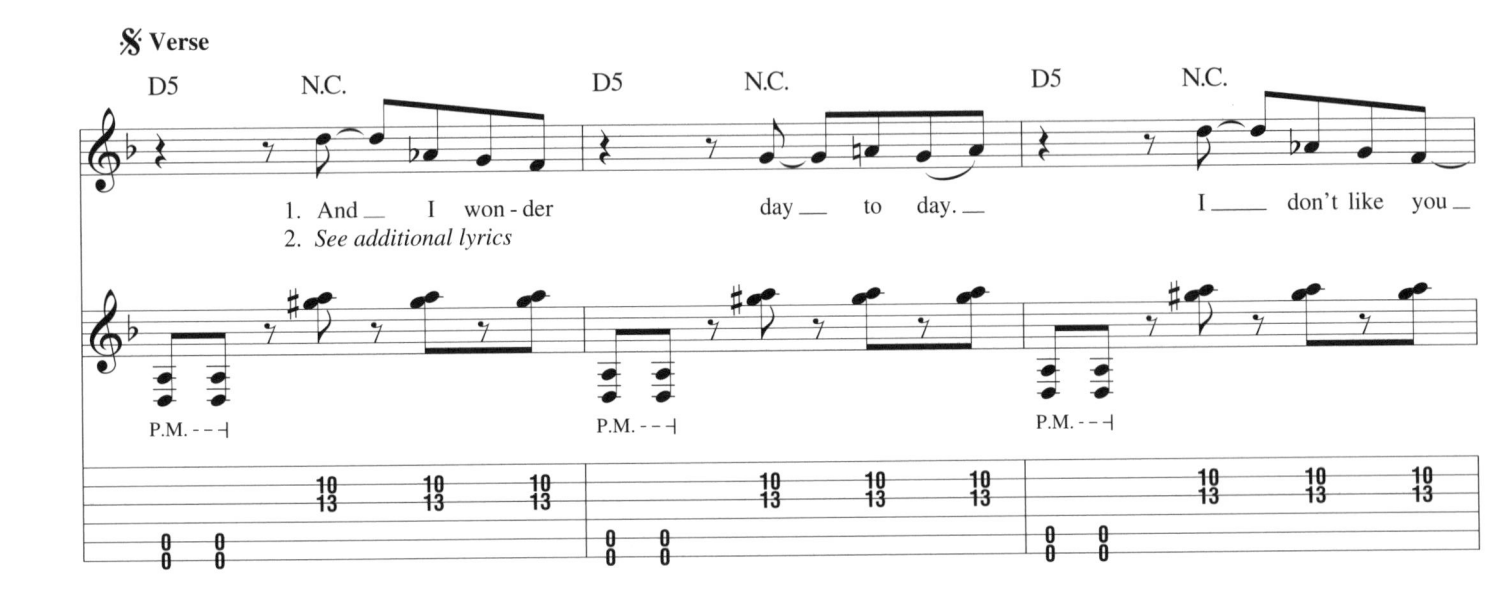

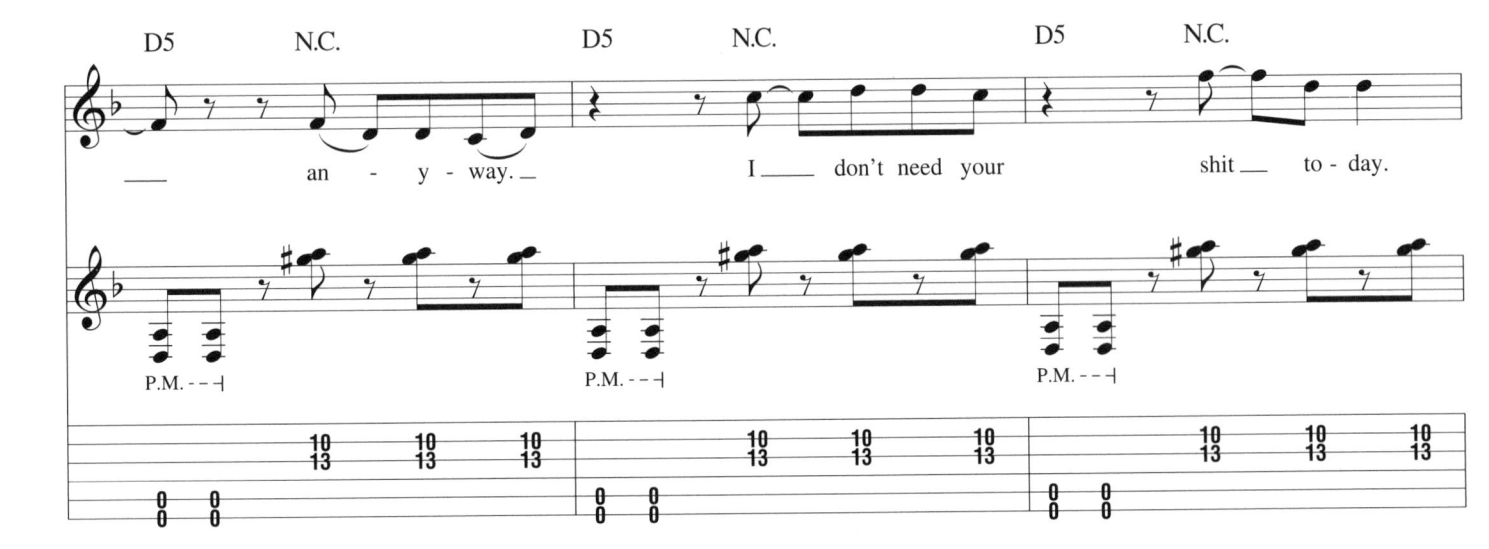

Bridge

D5

I'm do-ing the best __ I ev - er did. __ Go __ a - way. __

I'm do-ing the best __ that I __ can. __ Go __ a - way. __

I'm do-ing the best __ I ev - er did. __ I'm do-ing the best __ that I __ can.

D.S.S. al Coda 2
(take repeat)

I'm do-ing the best __ I ev - er did, now go __ a - way. __

Coda 2
Outro

Yeah.　　Yeah.　　I'm do-ing the best __ I ev-er did. __

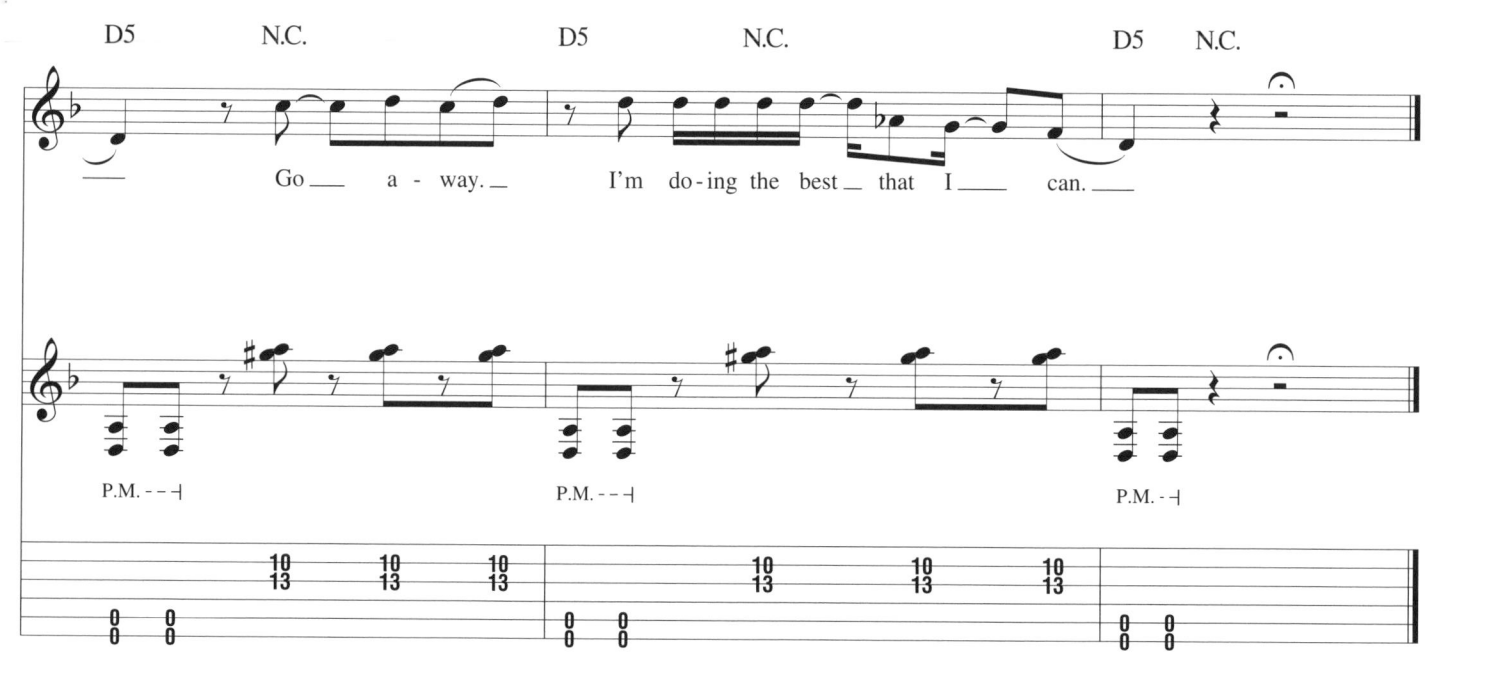

— Go __ a - way. __　I'm do-ing the best __ that I __ can. __

Additional Lyrics

2. I don't need to fantasize,
   You are my pets all the time.
   I don't mind if you go blind.
   You get what you get until you're through with my life.

Straight Out of Line

Words and Music by Sully Erna

Drop D tuning, down 1 step:
(low to high) C-G-C-F-A-D

Intro
Moderate Rock ♩ = 92

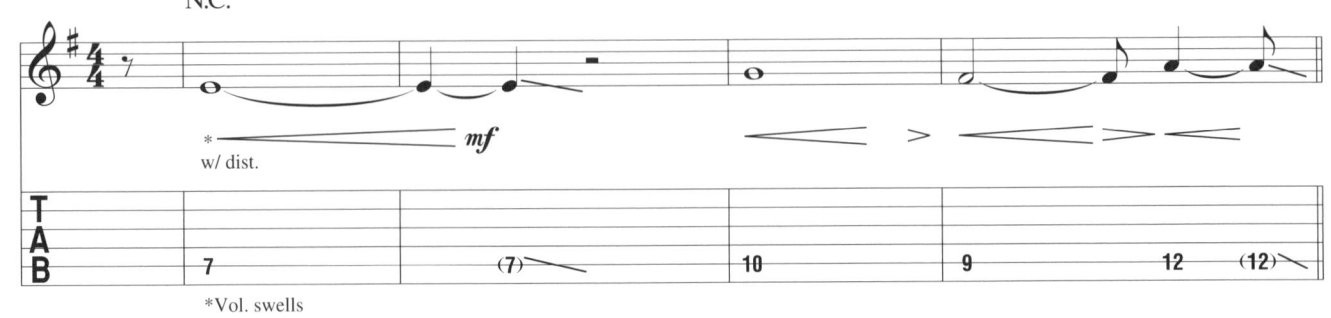

*Vol. swells

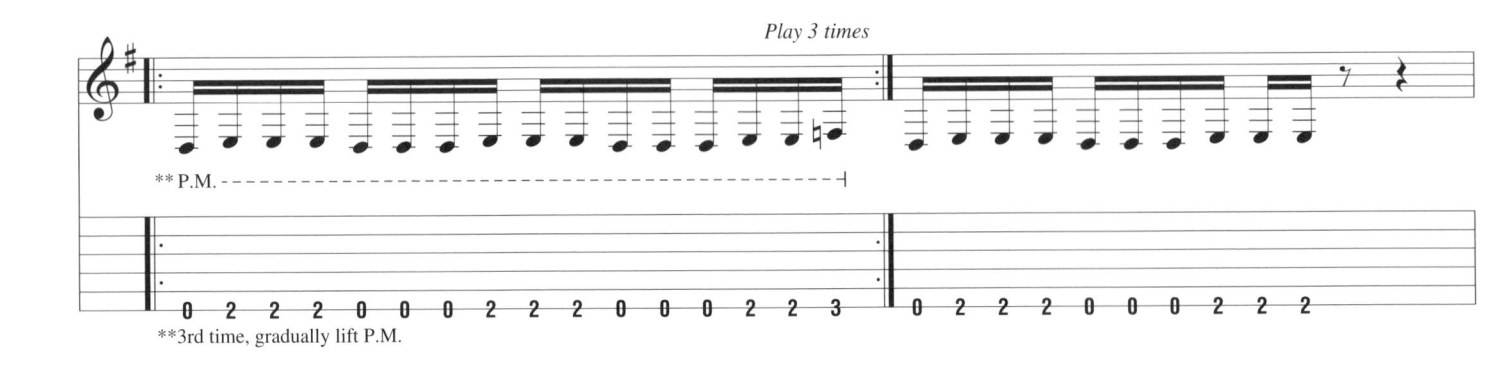

**3rd time, gradually lift P.M.

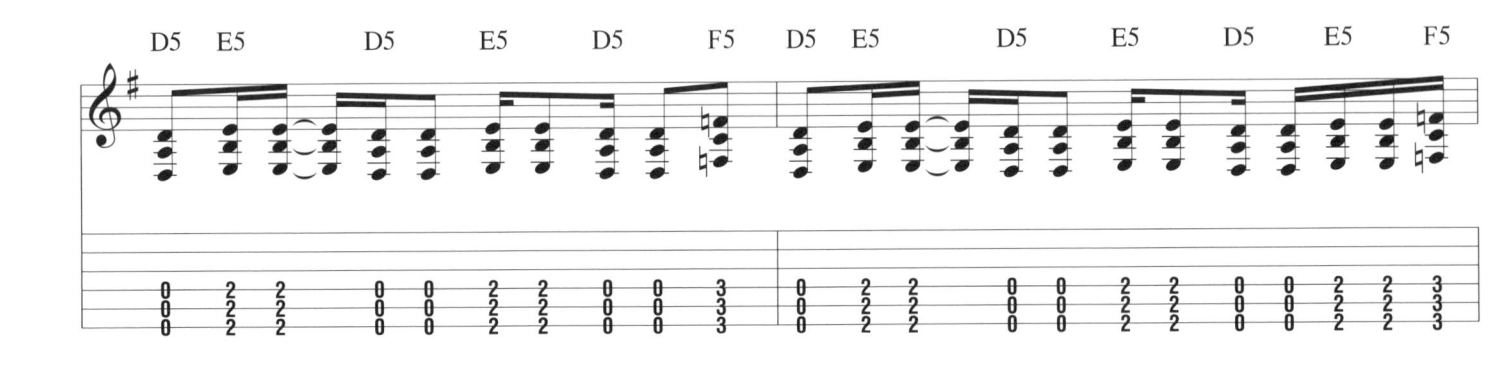

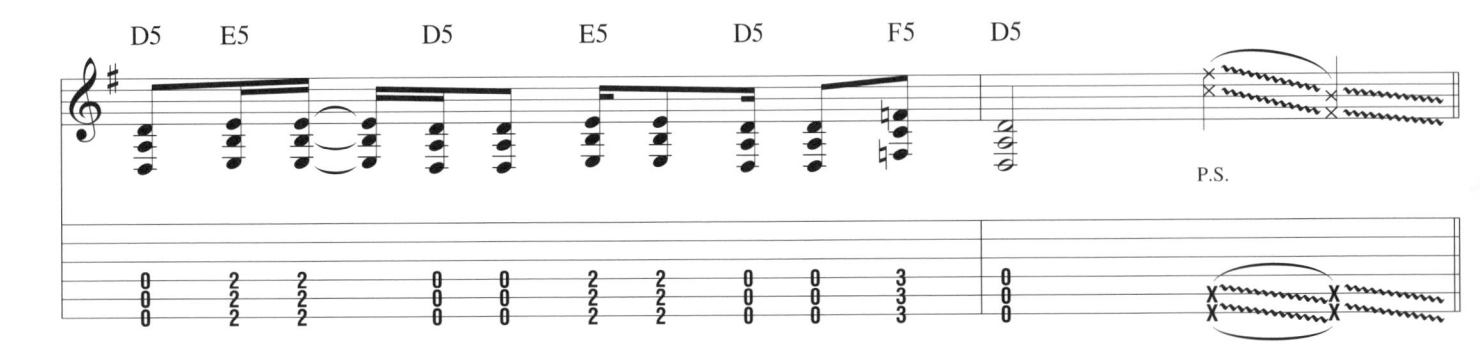

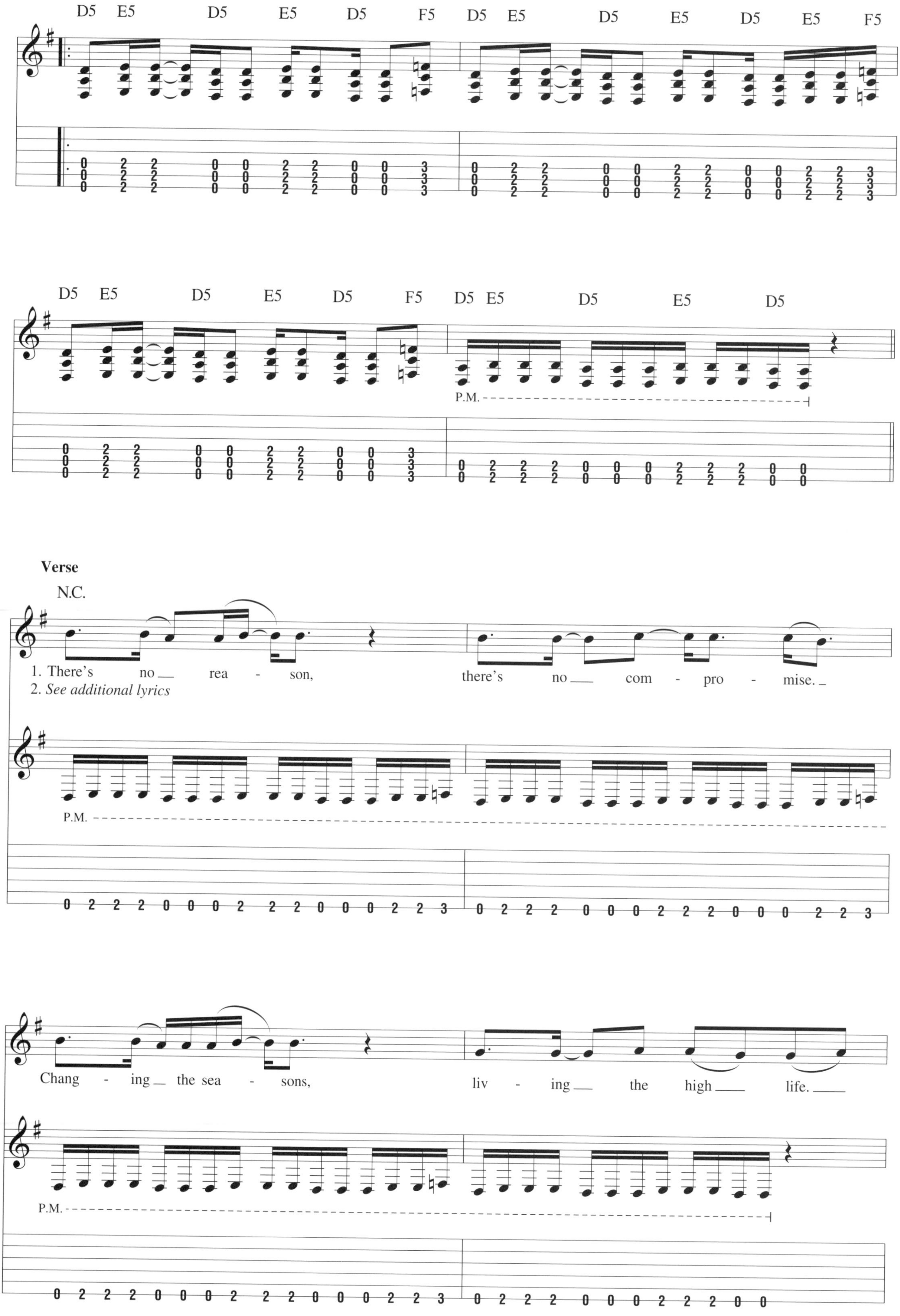
D5 E5 D5 E5 D5 F5 D5 E5 D5 E5 D5 E5 F5
D5 E5 D5 E5 D5 F5 D5 E5 D5 E5 D5
P.M.
Verse
N.C.
1. There's no rea - son, there's no com - pro - mise.
2. See additional lyrics
P.M.
Chang - ing the sea - sons, liv - ing the high life.
P.M.

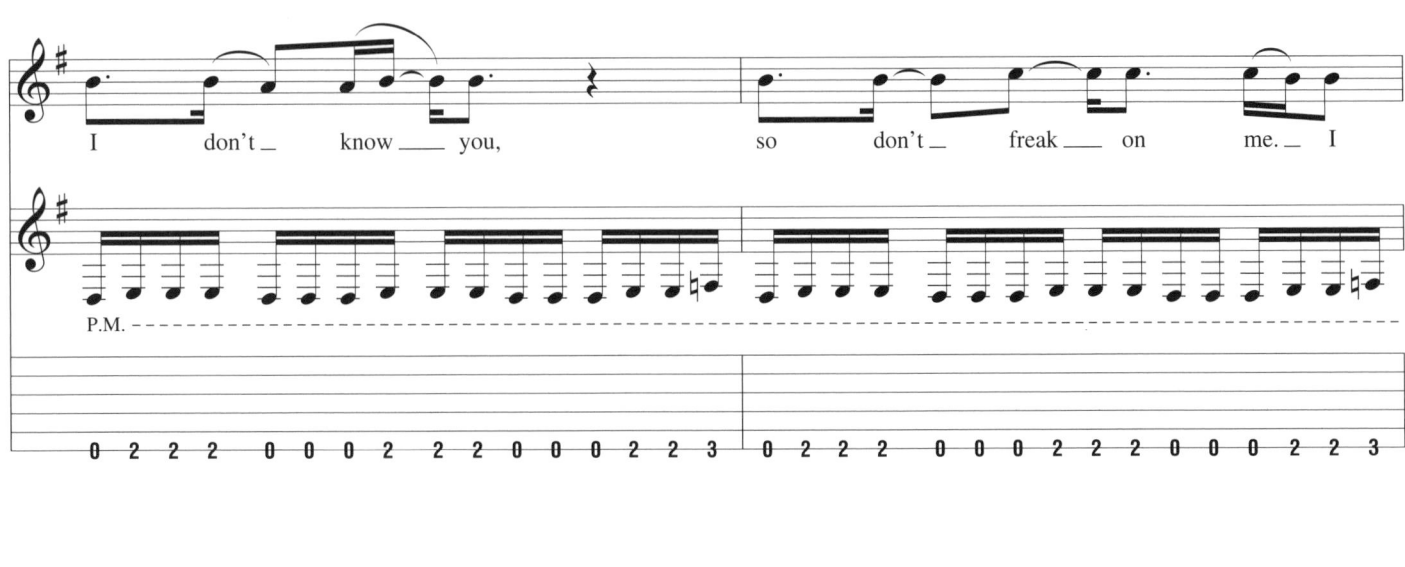

I don't _ know _ you, so don't _ freak _ on me. _ I

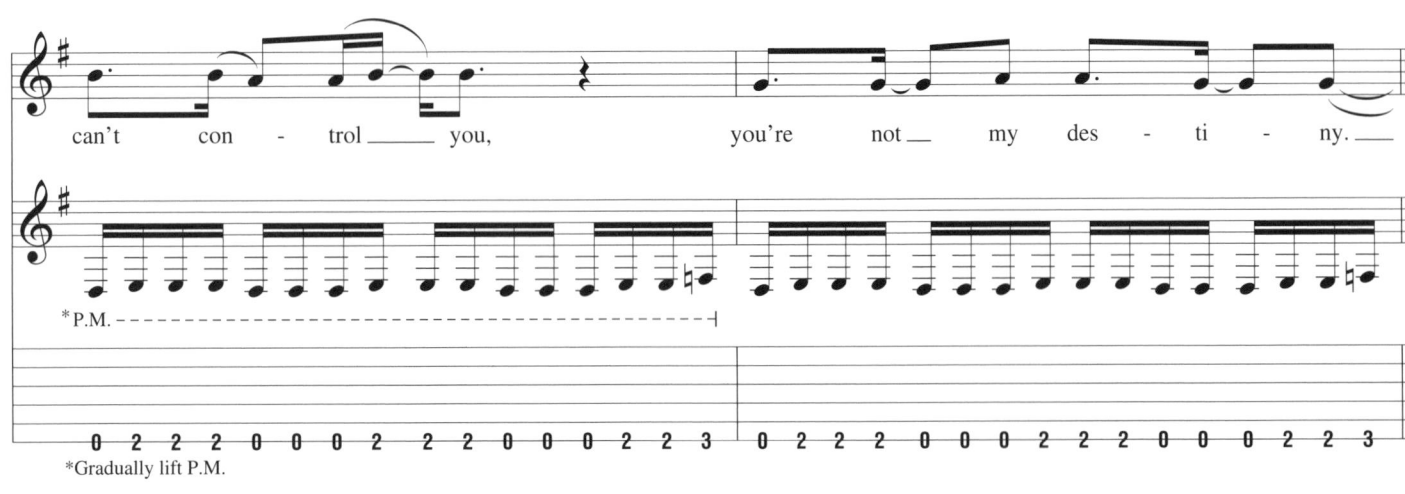

*P.M.

can't con - trol _ you, you're not _ my des - ti - ny. _

*Gradually lift P.M.

%Chorus

3rd time, substitute Fill 1

E5   G5

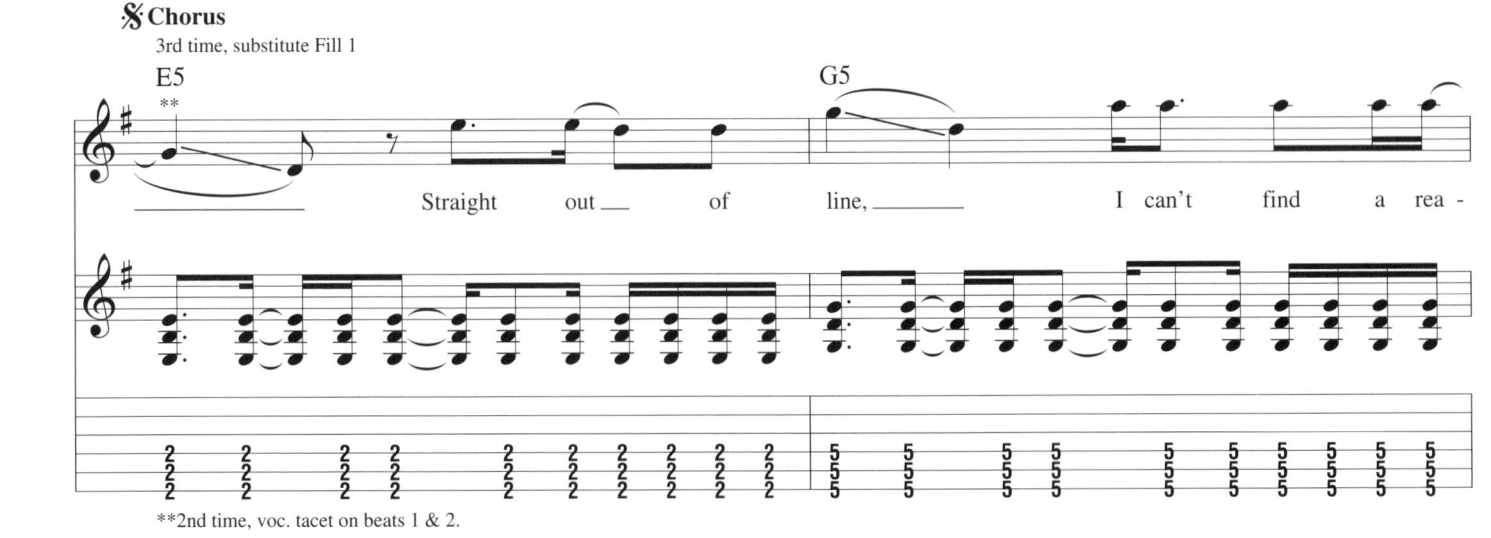

Straight out _ of line, _ I can't find a rea -

**2nd time, voc. tacet on beats 1 & 2.

Fill 1

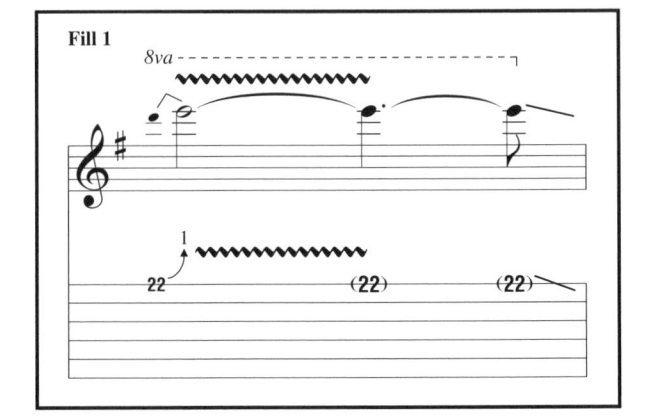

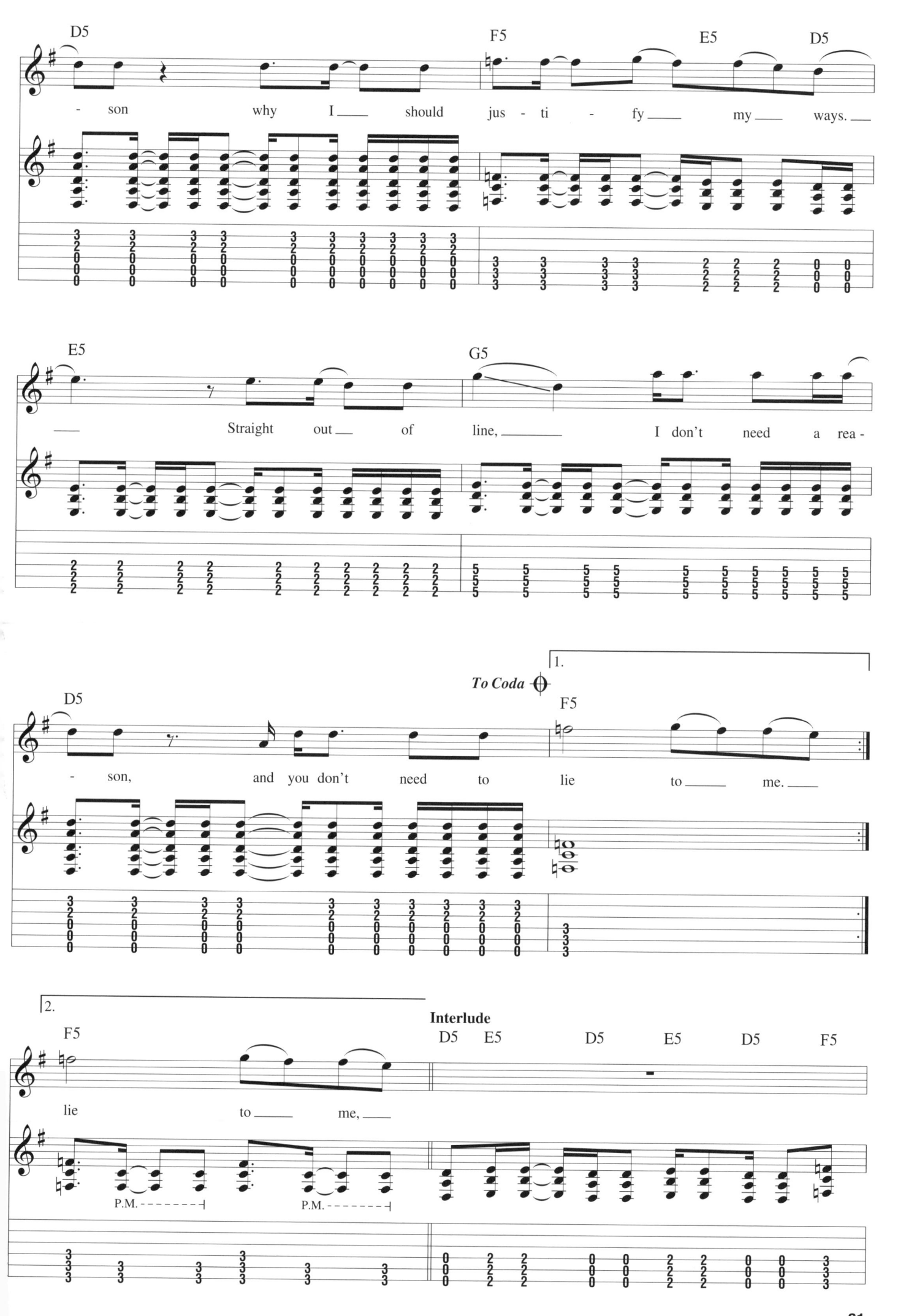

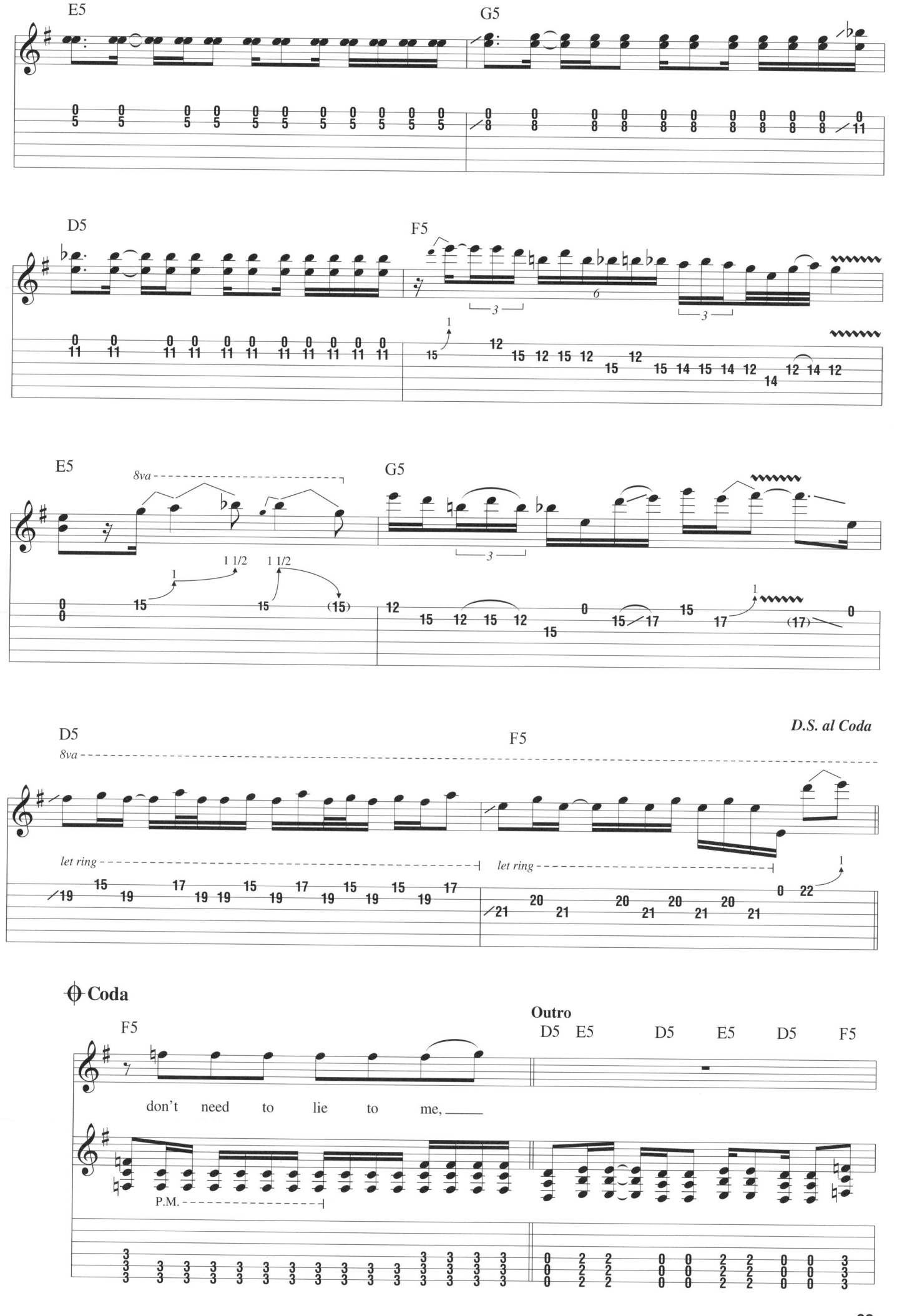

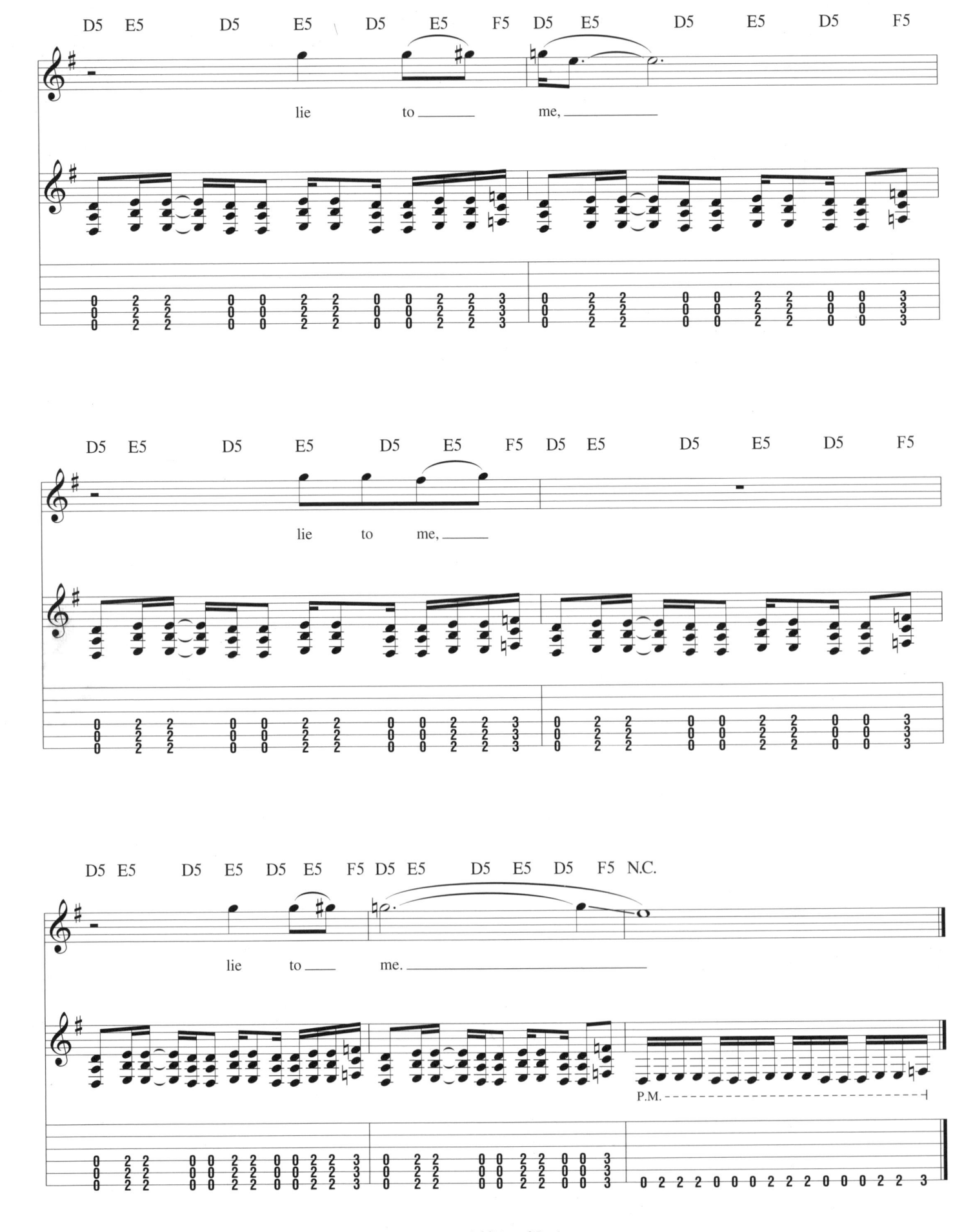

Additional Lyrics

2. I'll confess this, you're my tragedy.
   I laid you to rest just as fast as you turned on me.
   Gone forever, banish the memories.
   Displays of pleasure are masked by your misery.